Quiet
Pattern

Gentle Design for Interiors

Abigail Edwards

Quiet Pattern

Gentle Design for Interiors

In memory of my Dad

CLEARVIEW

An Introduction to Quiet Pattern
Abigail Edwards

In this age of maximum communication life can be overwhelming, and introducing pattern can feel as if it will simply increase the noise and confusion. But when chosen carefully, pattern can be as functional as it is decorative. Pattern can contribute to environments that promote healing, wellbeing and relaxation. In the field of healthcare, patterns are chosen based on the psycho-physical responses they initiate to create an environment that has a calming effect, lowering blood pressure and heart rate. Pattern can be illustrative, or abstract, dreamlike or very down to earth, bringing urban dwellers closer to memories of holidays by the sea or a carefree country childhood. Many designs incorporate the soothing colours of nature or themes from fairytales, removing one from the strife of modern life. Delicate and inspiring, this quiet unobtrusive aesthetic possesses a gentle strength, supporting but not overshadowing its visual allies such as architecture, space and light. Harmonious shapes, proportions and colour palettes can bring solace to a restless mind. Calm, quiet patterns can trigger thoughts and inspiration, allowing the mind to wander and create freely.

I used to have no interest in pattern at all. After training in fine art, I became an interiors stylist in 2000 and dreamt of living in a minimalist, industrial urban loft. The magazine that I was working on at the time was more traditional, however, and It was my job to style the fabric and wallpaper photoshoots every month. As I spent my days going through all the heavily patterned swatches that arrived in a never-ending stream on my desk, my appreciation slowly grew for all these beautiful, often intricate designs. It was a joy to select patterns that worked together, and slowly I learnt about the different styles, techniques and histories woven into them. It never occurred to me that many years later I would want to design my own wallpapers and fabrics. It was after working as a freelance stylist for about six years that I thought a little illustration of owls that I had drawn would be more appropriate as a wallpaper design, so I tentatively tried it out, luckily it worked, people bought it and that is how my business began. Working alone and untrained in textile or pattern design, it fascinates me how other designers work, how they run their businesses, how they create their patterns and what inspires them. I found it intriguing that all the designers I interviewed for this book work in completely different ways, yet all produce the most extraordinary designs. This book is an exploration of gentle, calm pattern; its historical roots and close links to nature, how contemporary designers work today and how pattern can be used in your home to enhance your space and to complement your ideals of serenity.

Inspiration and Process –
How an idea turns into a pattern design

Designers work in many different ways as you will see from this book, but here is a little explanation of how something that initially inspires me can progress into a complete pattern.

Inspiration is acquired from so many different places and seemingly insignificant moments, so it is hard to pinpoint exactly when the spark of an idea is ignited, or what makes fragments of a half idea stored for years in the mind suddenly come together. For me, it can take a while; a subconscious thought that rambles along a slightly neglected path over several years, before I am ready to start unraveling that intention in my own, rather painstaking and slightly inefficient way, into a pattern.

The delicacy of nature's fragile shapes are incredibly inspiring to me and growing up in a very rural part of the Cotswolds will always be part of me. When I'm at my childhood home in Sheepscombe, near Stroud, I spend hours walking my dog, in the ancient woodland that surrounds the village. Gnarly old trees fascinate me; the history that is captured within their branches hints at legends and secrecy. Many of my designs attempt to capture the unsettling but eerie beauty of the trees and fauna within these age-old forests.

I have made countless sketches of trees, feathers, leaves, plants and other random forest finds that sit in my sketchbook without consideration, waiting for the day when I will dip into it for research. Years might pass before I'll do this, but without intention or planning a new thought will trigger a mental image, and then the drawings become relevant, amalgamating and developing into a pattern.

The enigmatic and mysterious world of fairy tales that I loved as a child is another source of inspiration. I admire the intense detail and dark edge of Victorian illustrations from these stories. By contrast I also love the clean simplicity and graphic lines of contemporary Scandinavian design. I spent some time working as a stylist in various Nordic countries, especially Sweden, and have developed an affection for their folk tales, landscape and beautifully simplified design. Over time these disparate elements have fused together into how I create my designs currently.

Drawing is my favourite part of the design process. I will repeatedly draw something until I'm content that it looks how I imagined. The detail is important to me, but I don't like lines to appear too laboured, a little wabi-sabi is essential, and I would rather redraw something to keep the lines fresh. Having trained in fine art rather than textiles, I've taught myself how to create patterns in what I now realise is quite an impractical way, but this rambling approach works for me. I find the less digital and more laborious traditional methods a more natural and far more enjoyable way to work.

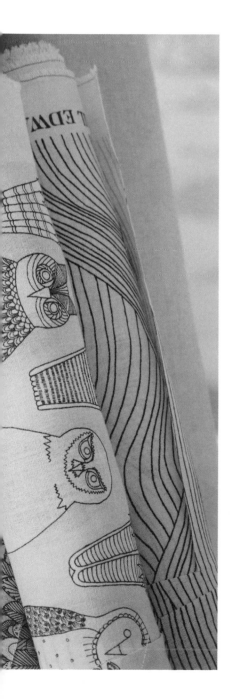

Brambleweb

I started drawing Brambleweb thinking about the tangled vines that protected the castle in the story of Briar Rose or Sleeping Beauty. I wanted the design to have a slightly ethereal feel whilst also acknowledging the darkness of the fairy tale, represented by the spiky metallic thorns on the brambles. The brambles are never ending, creating a protective barrier as though one was nestled in a bramble thicket.

As I worked on the repeat trying to achieve this protective web, the repetitive rounded shapes of the knots of bramble vines became more and more arts and crafts in style. This wasn't intentional but unsurprising, as at the time I was renovating a crumbling Victorian conversion built in the 1850s. The ceilings were held up with scaffolding and there was a crack in the wall stretching from the bottom to the top of the building that I could fit my arm in. I spent my days ripping up carpets and stripping off layers of wallpaper underneath which were the original Victorian designs. I tried to preserve pieces of the more historic papers, but they mostly came off as tiny fragments with bits of crumbling wall attached. I became engrossed, and couldn't help but think about who lived here in the past and how the original inhabitants would have decorated their home. Absorbing the history of the building during this renovation period seems to have influenced the flow of the brambles in Brambleweb.

RIGHT Brambleweb wallpaper Dusk on Nude
BELOW Inspiration and working drawings for Brambleweb

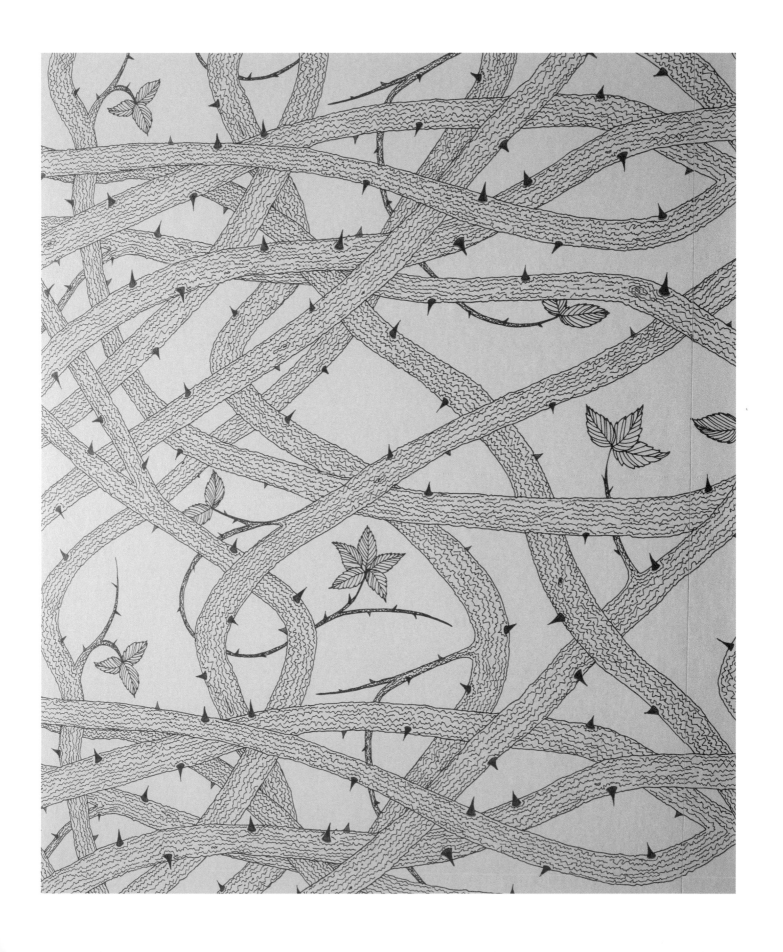

Seascape

Seascape was one of my first designs and one that is most important to me. I worked on it for about a year and a half, before launching it as wallpaper. I drew and redrew versions of the waves countless times to make them work as a subtle pattern that flowed seamlessly across the wall. I wanted the design to be calming without any of the waves looking clumsy or jarring, yet retaining a naïve hand drawn quality that celebrated its own imperfection.

The sea in North Cornwall inspired the wave design. I have visited Hawkers Cove near Padstow over many years with family, staying in an old converted lifeboat station that is built into the rocks of a cliff; when the tide comes up the lifeboat station is surrounded by sea. The atmosphere can be incredibly dramatic when the weather is stormy but very peaceful when the sea is calm and the sky is clear. The place is steeped in happy memories for me, and also a sense of loss for those who are no longer there with us. This slight melancholy is unintentionally echoed in the original colour ways of the design but this is also how the English sea can be, often grey and gloomily overcast. A few years later I wanted to introduce some more optimistic colourways, so I added Sunrise which has metallic gold lines on a pink sea to represent the sun reflecting off the sea and Dawn which is a subtle pink and blue combination of hazy mornings and pink light on the waves.

LEFT Seascape in Winter wallpaper
BELOW Working sketches for Seascape and photographs of the family holidays in Cornwall that inspired the design

Cross Stitch

My goddaughter used to live in Paris, and when her family moved to a new house I thought about designing a paper that could decorate her room. On a weekend visit, I found an old book of cross-stitch sampler patterns in a Parisian fleamarket. Later in the day I was in a favourite café in the Marais filled with second hand books and there happened to be two books on cross stitch on the shelf next to my table. This seemed like a sign so I spent a few hours sitting in the café sketching cross-stitch letters and patterns from this book until an idea for a wallpaper developed. I imagined a cross-stitch sampler in bright colours and sprinkled with animals making it fun to learn the alphabet.

When I got back to London I discovered some cross-stitching pieces that my grandmother had made. I started hand-drawing crosses to form the letters from the old samplers on to graph paper. This took days and after many attempts I photocopied the letters that I had already drawn so that I could move them around to work it out. Once I was happy with the position of all the photocopied letters and animals I drew the thousands of miniature crosses once again onto a new sheet of graph paper to make it perfect. This is currently my only digital design as it has 26 colours. Each alphabet and animal is a different colour, but the one shown is a more simplistic, clean-lined monochrome colourway.

RIGHT Cross Stitch wallpaper black on white
BELOW Inspiration and working sketches for Cross Stitch

Chapter One
The History
of Quiet Pattern

Prehistoric patterns may look abstract but those naïve lines are believed to be representations of the natural world.

The scratched and carved lines of the earliest pattern designs have been created with rudimentary tools and show that it is human nature to see patterns in the sea, land and sky surrounding us. I have chosen to cover only the periods of history that I felt were relevant to this particular style of quiet pattern, from the reaction to the mechanisation of the Victorian era, through English and Scandinavian modernism. These designers share a love of nature, an affinity for simple rural life and a belief in social equality. Similar natural themed botanical imagery appears throughout their designs, which are as relevant today as when they were first designed.

Arts & Crafts Aesthetic Movement

"Now if you should think I have got on to matters over serious for our small subject of pattern designing, I will say, first, that even these lesser arts, being produced by man's intelligence, cannot really be separated from the greater, the more purely intellectual ones, or from the life which creates both"
— WILLIAM MORRIS

The Arts and Crafts movement began in Britain in the early 1880's as a reaction against the long held establishment view that the decorative arts were inferior to architecture and the fine arts. Following on from the disseminating Pre-Raphaelite Brotherhood, and with an admiration for the critic John Ruskin, William Morris and his friend Edward Burne-Jones befriended artist Dante Gabriel Rossetti and went on to establish Morris & Co known as 'The Firm' with other friends with artistic leanings. Led by Morris but united by a desire to live a simpler way of life, and with a shared value in the importance of traditional craftsmanship they believed that well designed and conscientious domestic items could improve the quality of everyday life. With an emphasis on the domestic environment, they created everything from stained glass; embroidered tapestries, furniture, wallpaper, murals and textiles, essentially any decorative item, providing an alternative to the machine made imitation goods that were a symbol of the growing industrialisation of the time.

Commercial links were made with manufacturers enabling them to create beautifully designed items with the spirit of traditional craftsmanship, and bringing the ideals of the Arts and Crafts movement to a wider audience. Much of the patronage came from the architects of the Gothic Revival who unlike previous architects considered the entirety of the dwelling when designing buildings, including the contents and decoration of the interiors right down to specific items of furniture, textiles and fittings, making sure that the entire building and its interior were harmonious.

With a resurgence in the appreciation of craftsmanship today, arts and crafts style is becoming increasingly popular. "Their stylised forms and layered patterning, mean the designs work well in contemporary spaces, they are familiar and comforting at the same time being powerful and unique. They work particularly well in modern homes with exposed materials such as timber or stone and built with the same attention to detail and craftsmanship." Says Rebecca Craig, of Morris & Co. Design.

LEFT Previous Page: Acorn wallpaper, 1879, by William Morris RIGHT. Willow, 1887, by William Morris (both available from Morris & Co. Style Library)

William Morris
(1834–1896)

William Morris is arguably the single most important designer in British textile design history. Having started his career as an architect and poet before trying his hand at painting on the advice of Dante Gabriel Rossetti who said "If any man has poetry in him he should paint." He realised painting wasn't where he excelled and began to explore his talent as a designer and worked in a way that fitted with his socialist ideals and his aim of enabling social reform through the medium of decorative arts.

Not only was Morris prolific in his designs, he also revived long forgotten techniques of dyeing, weaving and printing in his own factory at Merton Abbey Mills in London. He revitalised medieval crafts traditions as a result of his aversion to the 19th century industrial age and a rebellion against what he considered to be the destructiveness of capitalist society. He was meticulous in learning both modern and ancient techniques of the manufacturing process before he started designing a particular product so that he could get the best possible results and understood the benefits of each method.

His interest in gardening and botanical knowledge fed into his designs, as did his love of the natural world, often featuring flowers, animals, birds and trees that he had observed first hand outside his houses The Red House in Bexleyheath and Kelmscott Manor in Gloucestershire. He describes Kelmscott as having a "sadness about it, which is not gloom but the melancholy born of beauty I suppose, it is very stimulating to the imagination" He produced many designs there and his daughter May continued to reside there for many years after his death, still producing embroidery for Morris & Co.

Rebecca Craig, Design Manager at Morris & Co. Design says, "He loved the craftsmanship in the creative process and believed this added to the quality and value of the design. The authenticity of Morris' designs resonates throughout his work. They are so complex and curated to perfection. Yet, there is room in each of his designs for a contemporary twist, making them relevant and interesting to today's market. People feel a comfortable familiarity with his designs. Morris' designs are iconic to the eye, bold and classic. The historical influences that Morris used in his patterns, gives them a unique longevity and beauty."

LEFT Branch, 1871, William Morris
BELOW Acanthus, 1875 by William Morris (both
available from Morris & Co. Style Library)

E.W. Godwin
(1833–1886)

BELOW *Bamboo Branch*, 1872 by EW Godwin (Available from Morris & Co. Style Library.) TOP RIGHT Sea Gulls, 1892, by CFA Voysey BOTTOM RIGHT: The Fairyland, 1896, by CFA Voysey (Both available from Trustworth Studios)

Referred to by Oscar Wilde as one of the most artistic spirits of this century in England, Edward William Godwin trained as an architect and was a respected critic, as well as writing extensively on how he decorated his own interiors. He struggled to find wallpapers for his home saying "There was plenty of bright colouring, but I could not find it anywhere combined both with simplicity and delicacy or refinement". He described the colours of the papers available as "where the tones were quiet they were also dull and unwholesome for the eye, where they were not quiet, they were not simply loud but uproarious". And goes on to say "After 5 years' endurance of this I was at last induced to design some papers for myself" His designs were paired down and clearly influenced by the simplicity and clean lines in Japanese art.

Godwin was part of the aesthetic movement, which drew designers and artists together believing that society could be made better through art and that art should be available to all and "Like Morris, Godwin was dedicated to beautifying the home whilst promoting a healthful domestic environment." Says Rebecca Craig, of Morris & Co. Design. Godwin may have inspired Morris as the willow was one of Godwin's most successful and favourite design motifs, used before Morris's Tulip & Willow designed later in 1873, although Morris' style of colouring was very different to Godwin's.

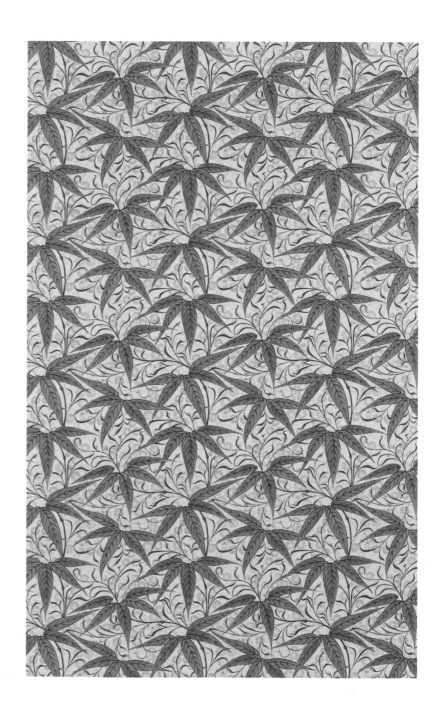

C.F.A. Voysey
(1857–1941)

Charles Frances Annesley Voysey spent his childhood between Yorkshire and London, mostly home schooled. He was unable to read at 14 and was a constant companion to his minister father, whose religious theories would influence the imagery of his designs alongside his love of nature, and a belief in a simple, honest and homely life. He worked as an architect until the onset of the First World War when work declined and then began designing tiles, wallpapers, fabrics and carpets as well as metal work, garden ornaments and jewellery.

Voysey was very conservative and even at the height of his popularity consistently undercharged for his work. He drew with 7H pencils and had immaculate draughtsmanship, using simple brick repeats in his patterns. He was inspired by the natural world and used his favourite motifs of birds, repeatedly. He reduces complex shapes to blocks of colour stylising the form, whilst retaining the characteristics of a species or subject. Using clear silhouettes, and strong outlines he depicts elegantly twisting and spiralling flowers, such as poppies, lilies and sunflowers bending in the wind. Some of his designs had moral subtexts, with a narrative on the battle between good and evil, featuring demons, and angels. But it was his patterns that showed an affection for nature and had a soothing restrictive colour palette that were the most popular.

English Modernism

The height of the Great Bardfield Artists' popularity was during the Festival of Britain in 1951 and like the arts and crafts movement before them they believed that art should be for all. These values combined with the influence of popular art, exemplified their version of English Modernism.

Great Bardfield, a small village in the Essex countryside was a hive of activity between the 1930's and 1960's as a group of artists descended. Having met at the Royal College of Art during what was known as the RCA's 1922 'outbreak of talent', Edward Bawden and Eric Ravilious hired bikes and explored the Essex countryside searching for rural scenes and agricultural workers to paint. They discovered Brick House in Great Bardfield, which Bawden rented as a creative retreat away from London and made his permanent home when he married fellow artist Charlotte Epton. Ravilious and his wife the artist Eileen Lucy 'Tirzah' Garwood lodged with them for many years and as more of their artistic friends from London came to visit, including artist and wallpaper designer John Aldridge, Bawden's student mural painter Walter Hoyle, artist Michael Rothenstein and Swiss born textile designer Marianne Straub amongst many others; several then moved to the village themselves, rejecting materialism and urban life and creating a thriving creative community of artists, designers and craftspeople living in pastoral seclusion. During the 1940's new artists came to the village to escape the bombing in London during the war, further developing the creative enclave.

At one point there were approximately forty artists living in the small village, many of whom moved into old, almost derelict cottages that became available as the local villagers moved out to modern estates. Despite the cheaper living costs of their rural location and although painting was their main passion, most of the artists needed a steady income to support themselves and their families. As a group they were prolific in their commercial work. Between them, making art prints, wood engravings, advertising posters, illustrating books, painting murals and designing tiles, fabrics, wallpapers and tableware as well as book binding, teaching art, making lampshades and horticulture. Blurring the line between fine art and design, they wanted art to have a social function and to be accessible.

RIGHT *Seaweed*, 1927, by Edward Bawden (Available from St Judes, Copyright of The Edward Bawden Estate, Courtesy of the Victoria and Albert Museum, London)

BELOW *Wave*, 1929 by Edward Bawden (Available from Common Room.
Copyright of The Edward Bawden Estate. Courtesy of the Victoria and
Albert Museum, London) RIGHT *Tree and Cow*, 1927 by Edward Bawden,
(Available from St Jude's. Copyright of The Edward Bawden Estate.
Courtesy of the Victoria and Albert Museum)

Edward Bawden
(1903–1989)

Edward Bawden spent most of his childhood "wandering around with a butterfly net and drawing". He studied Industrial Design at The Royal College of Art, which focused mainly on calligraphy, in his spare time he attended Sir John Cass School to learn engraving. His work had a strong sense of narrative and his paintings were full of patterns; rooms had wallpapered walls and patterned floors. He looked up to William Morris describing him as "an important chap" saying he wanted to "do lots of things covering the whole field of design as he did. He is still very much a hero".

Preferring traditional methods and not being interested in modernity, Bawden created his wallpaper designs with repeated linocuts, cut with a penknife. He stippled the lino with oil paint and used his feet to press them into lining paper on the floor. Bawden said, "I've no sense of form. I could never have been a sculptor. I'm a pattern maker". His early wallpapers were produced on sheets of paper rather than rolls, the size of the paper varying depending on the scale of the design. Later on he collaborated on a series of wallpaper designs with his friend and neighbour, artist John Aldridge, which were manufactured by Cole & Son, one of which was displayed at the Festival Of Britain.

He found more efficient ways of printing as he became more experienced and began to use a Japanese knife to draw, skilfully carving out the design in the lino. He worked sparingly, using simple materials. He was a keen gardener, swapping plants with other artist gardeners and illustrating horticultural diaries. After a scratch from a briar rose he lost the top of his index finger but this didn't stop him from working.

Bawden was prolific in his work, producing engravings, murals, watercolours, lithography and calligraphy and beautifully illustrated book covers. He continued working until his last day and died when he was eighty-six after lino cutting that morning. Kate Hawkins of Common Room, says, "Edward Bawden was one of the most significant artists of his time. His career spanned much of the twentieth century, and comfortably straddled boundaries between the fine and applied arts. His work was inspired by nature, often with a hint of the mythical, and with mischievous humour. Nostalgia and a love of nature are important. These are strong emotions. You can't ever completely quash them".

Sheila Robinson
(1925–1988)

Born in Nottingham, Sheila Robinson was an illustrator and an excellent water colourist and printmaker. She was a student of Edward Bawden at the RCA and despite a twenty-two year age gap they remained good friends for forty-two years. She moved to a village near Great Bardfield with artist Bernard Cheese, her husband, and after her marriage broke down she moved into Great Bardfield village with her two children. She would work from her kitchen table, with the children either drawing alongside her or playing on the floor. Despite this way of working her printmaking was always of an incredibly high standard, she would print everything by hand and sometimes by foot onto Japanese paper.

Robinson designed many posters, wallpaper and also stamps, as well as illustrating books. She made lots of observational drawings with imagery often inspired by local scenes and her drawing style had a strong link to the mark making in her prints. Her prints were mostly made with cardboard cuts rather than lino or wood so she could achieve more delicate effects. She would create textures in the cardboard base by cutting into the cardboard with tools that she devised herself and would tear off layers to create a relief print, the effect from the cardboard was much more textured and gentle with detailed lines. She would use lino or wood blocks for the areas that needed flatter, more intense colour.

Peggy Angus
(1904–1993)

Born in Chile and growing up in North London, Peggy Angus was inspired by both William Morris' designs and his socialist writings and, like him, believed that art should not be an elite experience. She won a scholarship to the RCA and would return home every day to use her family's knitting machine to support her art studies.

Angus was part of the same 1922 RCA group as Ravilious, and he and other artists from Great Bardfield would regularly come and stay at her weekend retreat, Furlongs; a shepherd's cottage in East Sussex with no electricity and one cold water tap. She drew cartoons on women's rights for the Daily Worker and, as a feminist, controversially defended her right to continue working and teaching after marriage and motherhood which was unusual for the time.

She was best known for her tile designs, fusing arts and crafts values with modern industrial production and wanting to humanise modern architecture with her colourful patterns. She had always produced repeats to show architects how to use her tiles so moving into wallpaper was a natural progression. She produced block printed wallpapers from linocuts that she would print onto lining paper with household emulsion paint. She ran a cottage industry from her home, asking friends to help her on bespoke projects, appreciating the visible brush marks and irregular markings on her designs.

Scandinavian Modernism

In the early 1900s there was a reawakened love of nature that was reflected in the use of stylised flora. Textile designers of the period embraced the ideals of a rural life, reacting against the functionalism that was prevalent (due to increased urbanization), and conscious of the need to maximize as much interior light as possible. The dark days and nights of winter had a major influence on Scandinavian design. As 90% of the population lived a mostly self sufficient life in the countryside at the time, home was an essential refuge from the harsh weather conditions. Later, as people migrated to urban centres, the ideals of living a simple existence close to the natural world remained. Making the most of the short summers necessitated spending much time outside, and heading to rustic holiday cabins during the warmer months became a priority.

In the 20th century, the Swedes stayed neutral during the war and many designers and artists emigrated to Sweden from Norway, Finland and Denmark as well as other parts of Europe. While industrialization came to Scandinavia later than the rest of Europe, the economy, unaffected by war, continued to grow, allowing for sweeping social reforms and the Fifties housing boom. Accordingly most Swedes lived in new, modernist homes, with value placed on craftsmanship, efficiency and a prevalence of mostly local,

natural materials such as wood and stone. Artisanship and practical democratic design were revered, with an appreciation placed on a humanizing approach over ostentation and luxurious detail. Most Scandinavians consider design to be an integral part of their everyday lives, a way to enrich domestic life. Houses were decorated in an understated but comfortable modernist style, bringing in textiles that contained small flashes of pattern and colour which echoed the colours of nature in a calm neutral palette.

This rich history of folk art, a love of natural materials and the skills of craftsmanship when paired with modern production techniques produced a style that was instantly recognizable. Sissa Sundling, Head of Design at Boråstapeter explains the enduring popularity of Scandinavian pattern. "Trends change over the decades, but this style is in our blood and these designs are part of our history. It's a way of living that is healthy and sustainable and it's this authenticity that makes it so popular and influences designers all over the world. The designers of this era created real masterpieces with very few colours, they were skilled at making intricate pattern repeats and they truly were artisans".

RIGHT Romans, based on textile design sketches made by Viola Gråsten in 1964 (Available from Boråstapeter)

Viola Gråsten
(1910–1944)

Viola Gråsten is one of Sweden's great textile designers, a pioneer. Born in Finland, she studied at the Central School of Crafts in Helsinki before moving to Sweden in 1945 because of wartime yarn shortages in Finland. She used bold geometric shapes and unusual colour combinations on all kinds of textiles, from blankets to carpets, creating hundreds of designs. She was designing shaggy rugs and then in 1947 began designing textile patterns for designer Astrid Sampe at Nordiska Kompaniet. This established her reputation for producing unrestrained colour combinations in her designs of stylized, sketchy foliage and put her at the forefront of a new era in the Swedish textile industry.

Gråsten drew inspiration from nature and was concerned about keeping the imperfections and spontaneous expression of her original sketches once they were transformed into pattern designs. Katarina Wiklund, designer at Bemz says: "you can see her artistic hand in her patterns, they have a hand painted look, which brings the pattern to life. The patterns are accessible and relatable, with a close relationship to nature, giving them a broad appeal".

Stig Lindberg
(1916–1982)

Stig Lindberg was born in Northern
Sweden and straddled the divide between
art and industry. He studied at the Swedish
State School of Arts, Crafts and Design in
Stockholm, initially wanting to be a painter.
In 1937 his designs began to be noticed and
he was employed by Gustavsberg's, one of
the most important ceramics manufacturers
in Sweden. He stayed there for several
years before setting up his own studio
and becoming an icon in Swedish product
design. But he returned later in 1949 to
become artistic director of the company.

Known mainly as a ceramicist, Lindberg
adapted to whichever medium he was
working with, tweaking his style to suit
the material. He designed television sets
and washbasins as well as dinner services,
glassware, sculpture, children's books,
wrapping paper and textiles. He adapted
his artistic ideas to suit industrially made
products, creating decorative illustrative
patterns with the whimsical imagery that he
is so well known for. He depicted a slightly
surreal, fairy tale rustic life; a Swedish
idyll of rural landscapes and hedgerows,
amalgamating into decorative yet elegant
folk inspired patterns.

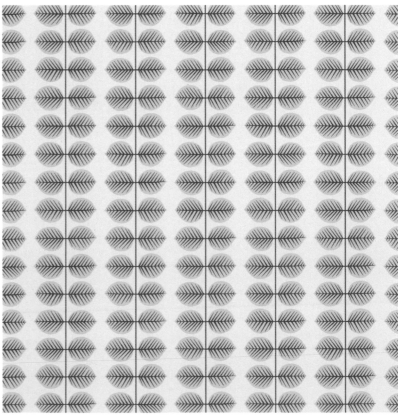

TOP LEFT *Grazia*, 1946 by Stig Lindberg BOTTOM LEFT
Berså, 1960 by Stig Lindberg BELOW *Poème D' Amour*,
1947 by Stig Lindberg (all available from Boråstapeter)

Arne Jacobsen
(1902–1971)

Denmark's best known architect Arne Jacobsen is famous for his functionalist buildings but as well as architecture and furniture he also designed textiles. Born in Copenhagen, Jacobsen wanted to become a painter but his father persuaded him to study architecture instead. He graduated from the Royal Danish Academy of Fine Arts, School of Architecture in Copenhagen in 1927 where he also studied furniture design. Studying both practical and artistic subjects gave him the flexibility to balance functionalist style with the softer organic forms of his most famous designs such as the Ant and Egg chairs.

During the Second World War he fled from Nazi occupied Denmark to Sweden. He lived in Stockholm during this time and spent his days designing fabrics and wallpapers. He painted directly from nature, using imagery that is a surprisingly fragile contrast to his architecture. He made countless floral textile designs, precisely drawn motifs of lush vegetation and delicate flowers inspired by Scandinavian flora. These were skilled decorative drawings, using naturalistic lines and organic forms. After the war his style gave way to more graphic patterns, in keeping with the clean edged ideals of his architectural design that he returned to in Denmark, although most of his textile designs showed a love of nature; flora and vines combined with simplicity.

Gocken + Lisbet Jobs (1914–95/1916–68)

BELOW *Köksväxter*, 1950s, by Lisbet Jobs (Available from Boråstapeter). LEFT *Bladranker*, 1950's, by Arne Jacobsen (both available from Boråstapeter)

Sisters Gocken & Lisbet Jobs lived in Dalarna, the heart of Swedish folklore, surrounded by Falun red houses, forests and lakes. The Jobs family had a studio and here the sisters' hand-decorated earthenware bowls and plates, with freehand painterly images of wild flowers and pretty weeds found in the surrounding fields and hedgerow. Their informal designs show a love of nature and folk art and were a celebration of rural Swedish life.

During the Second World War, raw materials became hard to find so they switched from ceramics, applying their floral designs to textiles instead. Their enchantingly spontaneous designs were a welcome contrast to the grey functionalism that had become a trademark during the war. Gocken in particular embraced silk-screen printing, creating richly detailed and colourful patterns adorned with wild foliage such as ferns, dandelions, buttercups and insects, whilst Lisbet painted motifs of meadow flowers and grasses as seen in Köksväxter, meaning kitchen plants, featuring various fresh green summer herbs in the sketchy style that is typical of her designs. They produced a multitude of textiles between them, including tablecloths, scarves, wall hangings and envelopes all epitomising the ideals of the Swedish countryside. Many of these were hand printed at the family's studio, the source of so much inspiration.

Chapter Two
Designers at Work

01
Daniel Heath

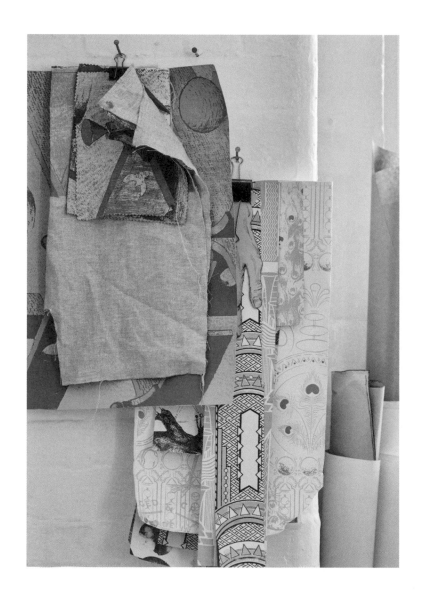

Daniel Heath—UK

Daniel Heath works from a warehouse studio in an industrial part of East London, UK, producing screen-printed wallpapers and fabrics, and laser etched surfaces and furniture. He uses a mixture of hand and digital drawing as well as modern and traditional manufacturing processes, to embrace the full scale of traditional English craftsmanship.

Whilst completing his undergraduate degree in printed textiles at Loughborough university Daniel discovered a local tea towel printing company were moving their production elsewhere. They wanted to sell their equipment cheaply to a graduate to help them get started. "It was old but really good silk screen printing equipment and I paid a pittance for it." This dictated the path that Daniel's life then took as he had to move somewhere with enough space for all the equipment. After a period in various live work units and having started an MA in printed textiles at the Royal College of Art he moved in to an abandoned jay cloth factory in Luton with some fashion designer friends to set up a studio. "There was loads of space, finally there was room for my 10 metre-printing table, and I started using the equipment properly. We would work all night, sleep there, it was a really interesting, productive time."

After completing his masters Daniel began printing for fashion clients, "It made sense to keep the studio going by putting other jobs through the equipment. Every time I tried something new, I got better at printing. The repetitive action of printing things like T-shirts was really beneficial, but I would take on unusual jobs too, which meant I needed to get specialist equipment and expanded my knowledge of what I could do in the studio. I was able to make a lot of mistakes and to learn things the hard way, which was ultimately good for honing my technical skills."

Daniel is now happily based in an old Victorian factory with huge windows in a quiet area of Hackney, East London.

"There have been people doing manual labour in here since Victorian times and when I am here printing I think about that continuity; the physical side of printing is quite laborious work and it feels good to be in a space that has that history. Previous studios have felt disheartening because the space has been blinkered or dark. Good light is really important. I need at least some natural light coming in. For about an hour a day the sun shines directly in, for a brief lovely moment. But even when it is overcast and the rain is pouring down, the big windows mean you can hear it all happening, I like to have that connection to the outside rather than being squirreled away. The journey here is also important to me as I cycle from home, along the canals and over the marshes, it puts me in the right frame of mind."

Daniel's delicate patterns are often based "on something substantial that I can get my teeth stuck in to." For his next theme he is exploring invasive species "I'm looking at flora and fauna that are doing really well all over the country because they don't have any predators." He is exploring the stories of how these plants and creatures arrived in the UK in the first place and the many directions that the design can take. "Sometimes I will land on something and have a eureka moment and other times I will develop something into a design and then it won't be quite right so I will go back again and add into it. Doing all the printing myself gives me that flexibility to make changes."

Initially Daniels' designs began as hand drawn images that were photocopied

and constructed into a repeat before
being traced and put on to a silk screen.
When he started he didn't know how to
use Photoshop or Illustrator, but finds
computers increasingly efficient for
scanning in hand drawings, scaling them
up or down and building up the geometric
elements to make sure they are precise.
He'll then add to the design by hand
afterwards, drawing into the pattern with
a chinagraph pencil, to create shaded,
textured marks and highlights.

Etching onto salvaged surfaces is
another medium, and the materials Daniel
uses are mostly found in reclamation yards
or in skips but sometimes belong to clients.
They are materials that if taken out of
context would be considered waste "Slate
is a really good material, largely unchanged
from when it came out of the ground, it's
gathered all this information and aging
over time that adds to the story, so it's
nice to bring that back around again and
reinterpret it in an unexpected way. I like
the balance of integrating a new technology
with salvaged material whilst maintaining
the ideology of a crafted aesthetic. Even
if the print or etching is digital, you still
have the patina or the marks in the wood
or slate, as well as the hand finishing of the
piece so that it has a natural quality to it".

As Daniel prints his work himself,
he is able to create bespoke designs for
clients incorporating something personal
to them into the work. He was recently
working on an etched panel with birds
for a bathroom and added in the birds
that visited the client's garden every day.
Another client wanted five different birds
to represent the five members of the family.
"If an idea comes directly from the person
commissioning the work you know that
every time they look at it they are going
to feel something very personal. I want
people to engage with the narrative as well
as the image, I hope it fires up something
in their imagination. At the same time, I've
succeeded in creating a unique design".

BELOW Daniel screen printing a wallpaper order in his studio surrounded by boards showing samples of his designs.

02
Hannah Nunn

Hannah Nunn—UK

NOTHING WILL MAKE
YOU FEEL BETTER EXCEPT
DOING THE **WORK**

RESPOND TO EVERY
CALL THAT EXCITES
YOUR SPIRIT
rumi

Hannah Nunn creates gentle patterns of grasses and meadow flowers made from silhouettes and paper cuts in her light filled studio overlooking the scenic town of Hebden Bridge in West Yorkshire in England. Building up a bank of images from trips with her camera and sketchbook in woodlands and fields before translating these into designs.

Hannah's life took an unexpected turn when, after having her children and deciding not to resume her degree at Carmarthen College of Art in Wales, she rented a shared studio. Without knowing what she would be using it for but just needing a space to be creative, as she says "I bought some equipment, a cutting mat and a knife and started paper cutting. I decided to make a range of hand made cards, something that I could sell." So successful was she that soon her cards were selling everywhere, but the economics didn't really work. It was while holding her paper cuts up to the window to check the light shining through them, that prompted one her co-renters to suggest she make paper lampshades.

With an Arts Council grant, Hannah was able to develop her signature style – paper cut with silhouette motifs for the light to shine through. But the repetitive strain injury caused by paper cutting drew her towards technology when she began using a laser cutter instead. So she completed an online course in surface pattern design, which really inspired her and led to the possibilities of expanding her range into fabrics and wallpapers. "Creating repeats in the computer is amazingly fun, and learning how to do multiples of a repeat so efficiently really appealed to me. Laser cutting is financially expensive and paper cutting is time consuming and physically demanding, so I really enjoyed growing patterns in this way, it was a revelation. Suddenly I could duplicate the design. There was an explosion of the mediums I could work on and what I could create."

With so many projects on the go, it was time to move. "I needed somewhere to spread out so that I could design wallpaper. I wanted a private space where I wouldn't be disturbed." Her current studio is a calm oasis, with separate areas for laser cutting, drawing, fabric cutting and a little showroom. She now employs a studio manager as well as her father who works one day a week, helping to make the lamps and wrap orders and there is often a student intern. "I had a vision of what I wanted my ideal studio to look like and this is it, I love the wall to wall windows. I look out and see the trees and I can see the birds on the building opposite learn to eat cherries in the gutter so that they don't roll off the roof. I love having a place to come to that is absolutely mine, where I can potter with my house plants and be creative."

Hannah's designs are made up of extremely delicate silhouettes of grasses and flowers that start off as sketches before turning into paper cut motifs, which are then arranged into a pattern. "Looking at nature up close gives me frissons of excitement, I immediately want to draw the delicacy. I am a sucker for detail and it matters to me that when you see each flower clearly within my patterns, it has its own detail." Hannah can name where and when she saw the individual motifs on each design. "I can remember the particular moment, when I saw that particular dandelion, in that particular meadow and I held it up to the light and thought wow, look at how that structure works, look at how the tiny seeds are held together. I can't wait to get back to the studio and begin designing."

Hannah finds her inspiration on walks around Hebden Bridge. "I always take my camera, I am continually looking up close at the things I discover. I draw in a sketch book when I am sitting in a meadow, my sketch book is quite big as some of the grasses are really big and I don't want to confine them into a small space, but generally I work from photos. I stayed at a perfect place called Wild Meadow this year. The house was within seconds of millions of different flowers and grasses. We did masses of flower pressing, drawing and painting - it was absolutely lovely." After these excursions she will come back to the studio and draw on bits of A4 paper. "I'm usually thinking about how I can turn a motif into a shape to use in illustrator, for instance, rather than just drawing for the pleasure of drawing. I will draw a shape and then colour it in to create a silhouette because that will make the best scan, something that I can cut out and move around. I start with a 52cm by 52cm square box and I play around with the silhouettes within that box to make the repeat." Her aim is to recreate the feeling of sitting in a meadow looking out over a billowing wave of pattern.

A recent commission from The Bronte Parsonage to design a pattern to celebrate the bicentenary of author Charlotte Bronte's birthday has resulted in Hannah's wallpaper entitled 'Charlotte's Garden'. Having seen her previous work, The Parsonage, which is a few miles over the moors from Hannah, suggested she make a design based on the meadow behind the house, but unfortunately it wasn't flowering at that time of year. The garden on the other hand was very much in bloom. "All the Alliums were out and the Hellebores and ferns, it was just lovely." She took photos of her favourite flowers and worked from those.

With Charlotte's Garden, Hannah pictured a darker palette that would have been used in a Victorian house. "When we first moved into my childhood house when I was four years old, everything was painted a very dark green. The hallway was particularly dark. I imagined this dark green in my mind, I really wanted to crack it for Charlotte's Garden but it just didn't work. I had been looking at Victorian pursuits because of the silhouette style of my designs and imagined a cyan blue, but it was too much, we mixed it down to this lovely soft blue, the gentleness really worked." For years Hannah had been working with light and shade in her lamp designs rather than colour so it was a significant and difficult challenge to choose colour ways for her wallpapers. "For years colour was very hard for me. Initially I had an idea in my head of a really neutral shade that was easy to live with, almost like a craft paper, so that the papers sat alongside my lamps and everything was coherent. The factory I work with for my wallpapers has a colour day; you are assigned one colourist for the whole day. The first time I went in we experimented with what the designs would be like in different hues. It was a tentative step into the world of colour. I was really timid having not used colour in my work before. I love colour but I didn't know what my tones were. We experimented with soft blues and greys and neutrals and I came away at the end of the day with thirty two colour ways and it was mind-boggling" Hannah prints with Gravure, as her designs are tonal, so she can do a lot with one roller, which keeps the cost down, changing the pad colour of the wallpaper to give different options. "I can think of colour in the same way as light and shade by printing this way which suited me really well. This process allows me to think in layers."

"I am a natural doodler and have always been drawn to patterns. I try not be too paralysed or buffered by all the amazing things that people are doing out there. I just want to be really focused on on my thing, and carry on being excited about all the new designs the natural world inspires me to create".

03
Brendan Young
Vanessa Battaglia

Mineheart—UK

Vanessa Battaglia and Brendan Young founders of Mineheart, run a multi-disciplinary design studio in Cambridge, UK. Passionate supporters of British manufacturing, all Mineheart products are made in the UK but frequent collaborations with international artists working in various media go beyond functionality, telling playful stories through their designs.

Brendan Young met Vanessa Battaglia whilst they were both on a student exchange trip, and both studying Industrial Design; Brendan at Plymouth University and Vanessa at the Instituto Superiore per Industrie Artistiche (ISIA) in Rome. Following stints in a Milan design studio and fashion manufacturing company Ittierre respectively, they moved back to England and started Studiomold, a design consultancy. In 2011 they launched Mineheart, the name inspired by the Shakespearian quote "Mine eye and heart…" symbolising their dual passions of a love for tradition and an eye for contemporary design.

Starting off with lighting and furniture, they only branched into wallpaper, rugs and decorative objects when they bought their house. "We couldn't find a wallpaper that we really liked so we took a photo of all our old books and stuck them to the wall with PVA. I took a photo and sent it to Elle Decoration. They featured it as a full page in an inspiration column they were running at the time, and people started trying to order it, but it didn't exist, so we thought we had better make it into an actual wallpaper," explains Vanessa. As more and more people ordered the paper they decided to add more designs. "Some are just photos from our travels. In Bruges we took pictures of panelling, bookshelves and wrought iron – they are still our bestsellers, and our most personal designs".

Whilst Brendan is more engaged with the 3D objects and development, Vanessa is more passionate about the patterns and decorative finishes. "When there is decoration or pattern it gets passed to me but we discuss all concepts together". She is always searching for inspiring artists that they might want to work with. These collaborations usually have an unexpected twist on a traditional idea, but they won't work with anyone unless both Vanessa and Brendan feel that they understand the Mineheart ethos. "We've recently collaborated with Chinese artist Jacky Tsai. We fell in love with his traditional Chinese techniques and references; he shared our vision of redefining classical ideas of beauty. Normally the worlds of the artists we work with meet ours in a complimentary and surprising way".

It was a natural progression to add patterns and decorative elements to the collection. They like the way wallpaper adds interest and depth, a layer of history to a new space, which is why a lot of their designs have a nod to historical influences such as the Renaissance and Michelangelo. "I also love the theatrical feeling of Tim Walker's images, some of our panelled wallpaper and other architectural inspired designs I think of almost as a stage set. With wallpaper you can create something that doesn't exist," says Vanessa.

The romantic Loveletter wallpaper features beautiful hand written script; whereas Panelling is a photographic reproduction, all designs in the Almost White Collection are toned down to soft monochrome. "We are quite minimal, but not actually minimal," says Brendan. "There is something about things from the past, that bring a feeling of warmth and comfort. It's familiar because it has been around a long time, and it has more depth than a new wacky thing."

When they have an idea for a new design, they will play around with the image - whether it's a photograph or something they have drawn in Illustrator – and put it into Photoshop, then a repeat. After this the pattern will be fed into an interior design software system and tried out in a virtual room, with furniture, rugs and other accessories. "We want to see how it will look in semi-reality, to see if it is suitable for an interior. It's an instant reaction. If it looks and feels right to us we will go ahead with the product. If not we won't. We question if someone could use it in a living space, or if we ourselves would use it in our house" says Vanessa. Brendan adds, "You have to ignore the logical argument of whether something is commercial or not and just go with your gut reaction".

Mineheart started off in a garage in Brendan's mother's garden that they converted many years ago, in a village very near to their house in Cambridge. However, as the company grew to a team of fourteen, they needed much more space. They have moved to a larger space on an industrial estate outside Cambridge where there is plenty of room for them to store all their products. This includes a packing and fulfilment area, space for their team to manufacture the lights and work on prototypes as well as office and design studios. They now have a business partner John, who takes care of the day-to-day operations of the company so that Brendan can concentrate on design and Vanessa can fluctuate between the two. "I need to have a positive environment around me, I can't work in a messy or stressful space," says Vanessa. Brendan alternatively is happiest working at night. "If the noise is repetitive, I can tune out but otherwise it destroys the process and ruins the moment" he says. "I work best from midnight until three in the morning when everyone is asleep".

04
Anna Backlund

House of Rym—Sweden

Anna Backlund designs whimsical patterns and products for House of Rym from their studio in a former fish shop in the old part of Gothenburg, Sweden. The brand began as a collaboration, merging different cultures and crafts, celebrating skilled artisans and preserving ancient handicraft techniques, to create a contemporary take on traditional product design.

Having tried studying philosophy and working as a interiors stylist for architects and developers, Anna's obsession with patterns led her to the HDK, Academy for Design and Craft in Gothenburg. "I knew from the moment I arrived there that I wanted to make patterns, the repeat adds a depth to an initial design or illustration and I love the challenge of working out complex repeats," she says. After graduating, Anna continued to work as a freelance designer, selling patterns to a Swedish textile brand but within a year she returned to HDK to begin a Masters degree in textile art

In 2011 about a month into her masters Anna unexpectedly received an email from someone called Rym beginning "Hello dear lady, I like your designs". The patterns that she had made for the Swedish textile brand had been spotted at a trade show in Paris and she was invited to visit Rym Tounsi and her partner Zied Youssef in Tunisia. Anna took along her friend and fellow designer Elisabeth Dunker of Fine Little Day. At the end of the week they sat down with Rym and Zied who asked if Tunisia had inspired them to design anything. "We had found so much!" says Anna, "we wanted to make towels, ceramics, rugs. Where to start? We were so excited and agreed on the spot to set up a collaborative brand that celebrated playful Scandinavian design whilst preserving Tunisian craftsmanship. We called it House of Rym."

Anna carried on studying for her Masters degree whilst working as a freelance designer, eventually becoming head of design at House of Rym in 2017. The partnership has been so successful that Rym and Zied have relocated from Tunisia to Gothenburg. "It's a dream job; they have so much trust in me and let me design almost whatever I want". Anna uses a variety of methods to create her designs, often starting from small painted illustrations that she will scan, or from naive paper cuts that she paints. "I think every method is a good way of working if something new emerges from it." A lot of Anna's designs start on sheets of brown craft paper. "I love this paper, it's very cheap and I already have lots of it, so it doesn't feel precious, I can make mistakes. Being an inexpensive material, I can fold it, and cut it without worrying, it's a really good way to start something. I am almost afraid to begin on an empty sheet of white paper. The pressure is too much. I have to move around it in some way and make marks on it so that it isn't so white and empty. I don't think of myself as a really good painter, but I have a feeling for composition and harmony and the distance between shapes and maybe for colours, for example subtracting things when the designs are overcomplicated, or adding to them when they are not. I'm not an artist that can sit and create a fantastic drawing on an empty piece of paper but with luck I can design a beautiful leaf, which on its own might not be much but when it's paired with another element it becomes something that really works".

To get started on a new idea Anna will observe what is going on around her, go for a walk, watch a film or sketch something. "The best thing for me is to just keep my hands moving, whether that is touching

some fabric to feel the texture, looking at colours in nature or drawing things I see on pieces of paper. It is not that I am super productive or feeling inspired all of the time but I feel it helps if I keep on doing things and keep my eyes open. I will often have a narrative running through my head when I'm working on something new, but it isn't important that a customer sitting wrapped up in one of my throws or looking at my wallpaper understands the narrative. It's more of a story for me whilst I am making the patterns, although I do want to give the observer a feeling of harmony and curiosity". A sense of longevity is essential to Anna. She sees the products as items that can be passed down from one generation to the next so it is very important to her that they are made from natural materials that feel pleasant to the touch and with patterns that give a sense of well being that are timeless, ensuring their continued presence in the home.

A lot of Anna's childhood was spent in her Grandmother's rustic summerhouse outside Gothenburg on an island close to the sea. Her grandmother was a keen textile artist. She built the cabin herself and filled it with Scandinavian textile art dating from 1920 to 1950. "The cabin was made of wood, it was everywhere. The walls were lined with wood but covered with traditional embroideries and weavings, almost folk art, hanging on the walls. A lot of the ideas I have come from recollections of here, as well as my colour inspiration, my colour palette is inside of me based on these childhood memories."

The cabin influence can also be seen in the House of Rym studio. It is in a former fish shop on a pretty street in a building dating from the early 1900's. Anna redesigned it to create a working space and show room. She painted the floors and lined the walls with wood. "I love the warmth of wood but also thought it would make a good backdrop for all of our products as well as providing storage that looks nice. Being in the studio inspires me, I feel very happy working here; sharing this space with the rest of the team contributes to the atmosphere of inspiration." Anna's designs for House Of Rym combine nostalgic and contemporary influences to create products with warmth and integrity.

05
Emma Von Brömssen

Emma Von Brömssen—Sweden

Emma Von Brömssen hand paints her designs for textiles, ceramics and wallpapers in an attic studio in her home in Gothenburg, on the west coast of Sweden. She uses various narratives to develop organic shapes within her patterns that work together and are subtly disguised so that each design contains a deliberate element to catch the viewer by surprise.

Studying design at the Academy of Design and Crafts at the University of Gothenburg allowed Emma to explore her interest in pattern, and by the end of her third year her enthusiasm for it was so firmly established that she went straight on to specialise for her Master's degree. Freelance commissions were a good way to supplement her income whilst studying, and she designed a collection of wallpapers as a graduate project. This became her first commercial collection, enabling her to launch her own brand seven years later early in 2014.

While working on her own brand, Emma continues to accept freelance commissions designing for multiple Scandinavian brands and if this wasn't enough, in 2017 she launched another brand Bliss, in collaboration with ceramicist Kajsa Cramer. Emma's designs are exquisitely reproduced on Kajsa's ceramics.

Emma runs her company from a little studio in the attic of her house. The light is good thanks to a skylight, which keeps the room sunny and bright "When the working day is finished, I can leave everything up there, not see it and spend time with my family, " she says. Having grown up by the sea and still living close to the coast today, its presence has been a constant source of inspiration for Emma. "I go there when I am tired or stressed. The blue of the sea is something that I always take with me. It's soothing and makes me feel calm." Emma uses a lot of inky, watery blues in her designs. "Blue is the colour that I remember from home when I was little. My grandmother used blue in her interiors

and we always had blue porcelain in my childhood home. It's a colour that feels natural for me".

Emma also gathers inspiration from the day-to-day. "I find new ideas everywhere - in nature of course. But I also see pleasing colour combinations when I'm out for a walk or looking through a newspaper. Inspiration is everywhere and meeting people and talking to them can also be really inspiring. My kids give me inspiration too". Travelling is a very important part of Emma's design process and she tries to go away at least once or twice a year to experience something different and to get a fresh perspective. "Travel adds another dimension to my thought process." Visiting Asia, and in particular Japan, China and Vietnam has had a big impact on Emma's work. "Each country is very different, but coming from Scandinavia, I can see the similarities between the craft traditions that we have and the ones that they use, the textile traditions are very inspiring". She is fascinated by the 8th century Japanese technique of shibori, the dyeing technique for creating patterns on textiles by folding, and twisting fabric. "I love Japanese textiles; the blue indigo dye used in their traditional crafts has always attracted me, as well as the delicacy of the ink drawings and how they paint directly onto textiles. I also love how they paint with wax". She is drawn to the centuries old skills of Chinese ink wash painting and brushwork. "It is very subtle and exact, the expressiveness created by the ink and every aspect of their drawings creates a beautiful nuance of tonality.

Emma uses a lot of ink and watercolour in her own designs, starting with a pencil outline before completing the design with delicate yet deft brush marks. She paints her designs on sheets of paper initially keeping in mind the specific effect that using a particular quality of fabric will create. Emma prints the textiles for her own brand on linen with a fairly rough, rustic quality. Once the watercolour painting has been printed, the texture of the linen creates a vintage effect, the tonal effect of the watercolour appears to be slightly faded and worn. "Unexpected things happen once the pattern is printed on to fabric, it changes the feeling and appearance of the original painting."

There are clever tricks within each of Emma's designs. She carefully considers how the various shapes work together and hides elements in each pattern to be discovered later on. Her Mackerel design began with some seaweed.

"I did some paintings of seaweed and noticed that the pattern on a mackerel's scales resembled the outline of the seaweed, the shape was really similar. I combined the elements disguising the mackerel in the seaweed background. I like finding solutions with shapes, and working with those shapes to create another dimension in the pattern that you can search for". Like her Crane design – from a distance the pattern appears to be a surface texture but as you get closer the birds emerge from the background. After looking at the pattern several times you will still find something new and engaging.

As well as her love of blue she works with a tonal palette of faded Autumnal reds and browns, all very natural colours. "Colouring is very important. I think it is colour that lends atmosphere to a space. Everything I do, is a combination of creating a pattern and colouring it to invite calm. I want customers to be able to use my wallpapers on all four walls of a room and create an atmosphere that is nurturing".

06
Birgit Morgenstern

Birgit Morgenstern—Germany

From a warren of rooms in her home studio in Lüneburg, Germany, Birgit Morgenstern prints simple yet bold silkscreen wallpapers and home textiles. Every single one of Birgit's bespoke designs is unique as they are developed in collaboration with her customers and hand printed to order. Her colour concept is sensitive and reserved, gently constructing an overall scheme.

Birgit studied textile design in Hanover in the 90's before working for a publishing house in Hamburg. After having twin boys, the family moved into a spacious house in the calm leafy town of Lüneburg near Hamburg. In 2003, Birgit rearranged several rooms in the house to accommodate her new screen-printing business. She took over two rooms in the basement, and two on the second floor. "I didn't plan to have my work separated over so many rooms, but the layout of the house dictated it. Luckily there's a lot of space and it suits how we live as a family".

In 2006 Birgit's screen printed wallpapers and curtains were exhibited at an art and trade museum in Hamburg and this is when her business took off in earnest. "I started primarily with wallpaper as this is what I studied for my diploma and I've always been fascinated in how pattern can transform a room. For me wallpaper is the most effective way of doing this. Plain rooms can lack atmosphere, whereas wallpaper adds warmth and personality".

As Birgit prints all her designs by hand, she is able to adjust the compositions to fit a client's requirements. She will alter the layout of a pattern to print the exact size arrangement for a particular wall (or a window if she's designing curtains). In this way the repeat will be unique to that precise wall. "I don't like to work with a regular repeat. Hand printing everything gives me the freedom to create a random pattern that is bespoke for a space. That's the advantage of being a small business and doing everything myself. I don't try to compete with the big brands, I work in a different way".

Lüneburg is a very pretty town and is surrounded by heathland. "My inspiration comes from looking at nature. I'll see something interesting and the idea will stay in my head and then a combination of other things I see, perhaps colours, will prompt ideas for new patterns". Birgit starts with pen drawings in her sketchbook or with photographs, which she then photocopies and scales up or down before sticking them up on the wall. "I usually have an idea of how I want to combine the pattern elements and I find being able to spread out the whole design on the wall the easiest way of seeing it in full". She then makes a collage of all of the drawings before putting everything together on a screen to print from, changing the line depth and colours to suit each client. "Screen printing has encouraged me to work in a more abstract way as I needed to simplify the colours I use. Three colours now looks too much, too imposing, I generally just use one or two colours, the simplicity works with my style and it keeps the process streamlined".

It is very important to Birgit to choose the appropriate colour way for her designs for each space "I will mix bespoke colours to suit a room. If a shade is too dark it can be dominant which might be what the room needs but on the other hand a lighter colour can fade to the background whilst also bringing warmth. The palette creates many possibilities to be creative. Mixing colours in the studio is one of my favourite parts of the process and when I feel most creative. The feeling of discovery through experimenting with colour is both surprising and rewarding".

LEFT A storage area in Birgit's studio where colour and pattern samples of her various designs are kept, colour experiments and inspiration are pinned to the wall. BELOW The showroom upstairs where clients can look through fabrics and wallpapers and discuss bespoke designs

07
Shanan Campanaro

Eskayel—USA

From an urban area of Brooklyn in the USA, Eskayel produce tranquil watery designs inspired by far away destinations to evoke the meditative experience of travelling to remote untouched locations. A love of the natural environment has created a strong focus on eco friendly design principles through innovative processes, materials and artistry.

Shanan Campanaro fell into designing wallpaper by chance. Having graduated from Central St Martins in London with a degree in fine art, she returned to New York as a freelance designer, and was invited to exhibit some of her artwork at a charity exhibition. She'd designed some patterned backdrops to hang behind the paintings on display, which were spotted by a local printer who recommended she print them onto wallpaper. As she was moving into a new house at the time, she decided to go ahead and do exactly that. The deluge of compliments from visitors who saw her living room encouraged her to start creating an entire collection, and in 2008 Eskayel was launched.

While the initial brief focused on wallpaper, it wasn't long before textiles followed, and after having licensed a design to a rug company, which sold spectacularly well, Eskayel rugs were launched in 2013. Now Shannan also collaborates with ABC Carpet & Home in New York on a range of cotton bedding as well as commissions from other companies on everything from phone cases to active wear to beautiful custom made furniture.

After years of working out of her loft apartment, which they outgrew, Shanan moved the team into a former clothing retail shop, which they have transformed into a beautiful open plan space. Walls were knocked down, floors redone, and a kitchen area added. They constructed everything themselves and Shanan commissioned bespoke furniture to complete the look. Shanan works at a big desk that she shares with her two designers in the studio/office area and two sales staff have desks overlooking the showroom area where customers can come in and browse the products. "It made sense to combine a showroom with a studio space and we have great light here, which is really important, not only for designing but also for production. We need to be able to see how the colours look together for colour matching wallpaper to fabric and when we are picking colours for rugs".

Eskayel's designs all have a tranquil watery feeling. Shanan has a very deep attachment to the sea "I am very connected to water. I live right by the river. New York is an island so I am basically in the middle of the sea and I can feel that. Even when I paint I am thinking about water, it plays a really important part in our creative process, I usually soak the paper to get it super wet and I paint with really watered-down ink in layers, letting it dry and then I wet it all over again and paint on top. I like it really messy, a little bit haphazard but in a controlled way. I have learnt how to control the bleeding of the inks into one another."

Shanan's designs for Eskayel are mostly inspired by travelling and the nature she sees whilst away, she tries to go on between five to ten trips a year and takes lots of photos. She then sits down in the studio when she is back in New York to work out which photographs she is inspired to paint from. "I'm really into travelling anyway, it's my favourite thing to do. I usually plan trips to places I've never been. I go somewhere to find inspiration. I like remote places that are a little bit untouched by people; obviously I love the ocean and

I love the beach and the colours of the sunset, I'm a big surfer.

I also love plants, I love to garden and I have tons of house plants, I've created a lot of work based on tropical coastal areas and tropical plants and I feel like I have really explored my tropical location paintings. My two latest collections are more inspired by cities I have visited. I went to Morocco and I was really inspired by the rooftops of Marrakesh and the light at twilight. The previous collection was based on my home town of San Diego."

Shanan will make paintings from the photographs that she finds most interesting and then works from these to create the final design. "How I work is always a little different depending on the collection. Sometimes I will paint little elements and put them together on the computer or sometimes I will use small pieces of a larger painting to create a pattern. The last two collections I did almost like a collage. I took a couple of paintings and merged them together to make a pattern, for my latest design I took elements of a painting and moved them around and reassembled them. I scan them in and cut them up digitally, I don't change the original work, as I like to save my paintings. We are doing murals now, so this is a different way of working again, the paintings get blown up and turned into giant wallpaper murals".

As for mood, "I try to evoke the moment I took the original photograph and recreate that emotion. I think of it as a visual language, so you can look at the painting or pattern design and understand a feeling without having to read about it. The sense of how you feel when you are relaxing on holiday, or sitting by the beach. Sometimes a sense of drama or melancholy that you might feel when looking at a sunset or a twilight, maybe a sense of nostalgia or a sense of place. A positive feeling that creates a positive environment, with a sense of tranquillity".

08
Sidonie Loiseleux

Sidonie Studio—USA

Sidonie Loiseleux's subtle white wallpapers are made from unfolded origami photographed in her studio in Echo Park, Los Angeles, USA. The designs are created by revealing animal patterns from unfolded papers. The qualities of the individual papers are carefully considered and how they will react to light once the creases are undone.

Whilst completing a fine art degree at the École Nationale Supérieure des Beaux-Arts in Paris Sidonie Loiseleux went on a 6-month exchange at California Institute of the Arts. So productive was the course, that after graduation she returned to LA to do an MFA in photography. After meeting her husband she decided to stay in LA permanently to work as a freelance surface designer while continuing to study.

One day after an exhibition she'd participated in, she was left with multiple sheets of display paper. Whilst experimenting she unfolded some and photographed them, took sections and manipulated them digitally before putting them into repeat. "I realised I had something. It was the first time I could combine my art with my job in a way that had meaning to me".

Her intention was to create wallpaper based on the material and concept of the paper itself. "I experimented and tried to work with the warmth and scale of the paper; the pattern is dictated by the delicate marks of the paper unfolding". Sidonie researches origami patterns for different animals and makes versions that she then unfolds, before deciding which one works best.

The wallpapers are often named after the origami pattern that they have been inspired by. Using the entire unfolded pattern Sidonie chooses animals that are significant to her. "I love the fox, an animal I used to get very excited about seeing when I was a child. Personal memory fires my imagination and I hope other people respond similarly".

She also pays attention to how the paper will take light. "Printer paper for example lacks character, some paper has too much grain, and some reflects the light too much, making the design too dramatic. I find heavy tracing paper works really well. One design, Elephant, is made with silver writing paper, it's radiant with light and reflects well so there is a nice gradient on the soft grey." She will either photograph or scan the unfolded papers, depending which technique works best with that particular design. "Scanning can occasionally be too flat, but photography can be too dramatic. I try to use natural lighting, to keep gentle shadows on the paper. Subtlety is important".

Sidonie's new collection is based on woven papers. "I want to challenge myself but also to have something new for clients. I want to keep working with paper but push it further. I'm trying out different weaving techniques, experimenting with squared paper and thinking about introducing colour". The new designs are named after various women who have inspired Sidonie. "I was thinking of how people are woven into each others lives and how that affects you, the people who have influenced me most just happen to have been women". Mattio is her mother's nickname; Alice is her grandmother and Doro is the friend who pushed her into going to art school.

Sidonie rents a studio about ten minutes away from her home. "I'm like a sponge, I absorb a lot of things and when I arrive in the studio I have a chance to process it all in my own space. I need that tranquillity I want this to come across in my designs".

LEFT A seating area in the studio with samples of Elephant and Whale hanging above BELOW An inspiration wall and some artwork by Sidonie's son.

09
Rebecca Atwood

Rebecca Atwood—USA

Rebecca Atwood transforms her sketchbook paintings into calming textile designs in her warehouse studio in Brooklyn, USA with an emphasis on ethically made production methods to create beautiful functional products. The process is as important as the finished design, prioritising time spent gathering inspiration and experimenting with techniques.

After studying painting at Rhode Island School of Design, Rebecca quickly found a job designing home ware products at Anthropologie. "I realised that designing textiles was the closest thing I could do to painting and get paid, Anthropologie was my training ground. I learnt really efficient techniques on the job and was designing everything from cups and bowls to kitchen and bed linen. I loved the creative freedom but we designed things that were a little more over the top than my style, whereas I fall somewhere in the middle." Rebecca then moved to New York to work with a design consultancy working for everyone from Amazon to Kate Spade. She travelled a lot, learning about production and getting a bigger understanding of the industry; becoming more familiar with the whole process of designing a collection, producing it and then selling it on to a retailer. "But I got tired of it. I felt like I was designing products to fit empty trends. It didn't feel personal and I didn't have a say in how or where things were produced. Sometimes I didn't feel the decisions being made were the best choice". It was time for a change so Rebecca took a break and started her own line. "I wanted to find my own story and the product to represent that visually. I wanted it to be a reflection of who I am and what I can do on my own. I'm passionate about pattern, but calm, liveable pattern".

She started small with about sixty cushions in total across several styles. Hand painting, printing and dying the one-of-a-kind cushion covers herself in her apartment, whilst getting the sewing done locally in the garment district. "I wanted to make things that felt more personal, to get back to having a studio practice, where I could work on things that were interesting to me and creating products that I wanted to have in my own home".

To begin with Rebecca worked from her two-bedroom apartment, dyeing fabric and washing silk screens in the bathtub. The second bedroom was a studio of sorts, as was the kitchen, shipping was done from the living room and pillow inserts were stored in the main bedroom. "At one point we had 100 pillow inserts in our bedroom and we couldn't get in to bed. I was working constantly because everything was always there. I didn't stop, it really wasn't good for me". After employing a member of staff to help, Rebecca relocated to a studio within a complex of old warehouse buildings in Brooklyn. As the team grew further, they moved to a larger sunnier studio in the same building. "It was really important to me that we had a lot of natural light so that I can see colours properly. This is a challenge to find in New York, lots of the spaces that I saw only had a tiny window". They added lots of built in storage to keep the space organised. "I don't want to see everything all the time and the storage really helps keeps my mind clear. I will always want more wall space to pin everything up, but we have a good set up. Besides the natural light, we have two large worktables and being able to spread everything out is great. It makes a happy, relaxed space".

Rebecca starts each new collection with a mood board, collating imagery and photographs that she has taken "I hold on to a lot of things, some of the photos were taken when I was ten years old. I pull a colour palette, usually just something I am feeling at the time. I will also look through my sketchbook. I feel that it is important to make time to just make things and not to know what they are going to be. When I go back to those sketches later on they will spark an idea, I pull them together and if the combination looks interesting they will go on the board. Sometimes I will make new things to tie it all together but often a lot of it is already made, although they might need to get fleshed out further. For example if it is just a motif I will need to make a painting around that to develop it. I rely a lot on the archive of things that I am always making". Rebecca is constantly painting in her sketch book, usually carrying one with her, leaving a couple at home and a couple in the studio. "I have them stashed everywhere. I get impatient. I don't want to have to wait for the paint to dry before I can turn the page. When I get a whole day devoted to sketch books that is amazing but usually I will get ideas on a bus ride or whatever it may be".

A lot of Rebecca's inspiration comes from Cape Cod, where she grew up and still visits a couple of times a year. "It is important to me to spend time in nature and travel. When you get out of your environment you see things differently. But New York is an influence too. I have been here nearly 10 years and it's part of me. I have a lot of creative friends based here; there are so many museums and exhibits and always so much going on. These everyday experiences and memories filter through the sketchbook and into a finished product. I think in terms with what feels relevant to me. I try to avoid following trends as much as I can, it's a backlash to my previous work but as a creative you are in tune with what is going on, you feel something in the air- osmosis". Rebecca's current collection is based around yoga

poses. The designs began as patterns that she had already made but the idea clicked into place whilst at a yoga class. "I was thinking about a collage I had made previously and it reminded me of the cat and cow poses and I started thinking about how we could create patterns that move together in some way" This was a means of tying the collection together without wanting to be too prescriptive. "I like that there is a bit of interpretation, I definitely have ideas about what the story is, but that can be abstract. There are multiple inspirations for each thing".

The colour palette for the first collection was mostly blues "This is the influence of growing up in a small coastal town where it is very quiet. In the winter everything is very muted, but the muted tones can be colourful at the same time. A lot of the colours we use that I consider to be neutrals come from that. I pick personal colours that resonate within the kind of environment we want to create. It's fun, helping someone to realise they can use a colour like tangerine or red as a neutral. When people think of red they think of the brightest red and there are so many other levels of red in between. I try to build on our colour palette as an evolution, so that something from our first collection will go with our current collection".

Once a design is finished, Rebecca will bring it home "I look at everything outside of the studio, in the studio it can be interesting conceptually but it might not work in a real home. With wallpaper we have to think about how it will look if it covers a whole room and how it will make someone in the room feel. Our goal is to be calming. We do have some bolder designs but they are bolder within a spectrum. Living in a busy city I crave the calm of my childhood and the washed through blues and greys that I grew up with. That is something that I am always drawn to when making things. That desire is so strong it comes into everything I do".

10
Kim Rosen

Fayce Textiles—USA

From an old factory building-overlooking mountains in a small town in Maine, USA, Kim Rosen of FAYCE Textiles turns her intricate charcoal line drawings of architectural facades, rocky coastline and weathered wood into abstract richly textural patterns that play with positive and negative space for embroidered and printed textiles and wallpaper.

After three years in the advertising and graphic design world Kim decided to apply for a Masters in illustration at the Savannah College of Art and Design. As soon as she graduated she began working on a wide range of commissions for The New Yorker, Wall St Journal and The Boston Globe amongst others. The deadlines were often very short, just a day or sometimes a couple of hours. "The pace was so quick. It was great for a long time but my passion wasn't there and I got burnt out. I wanted to create something that had longevity; that people considered and took time to choose. I wanted to know that If someone chose one of my designs, it would become part of their lives - less fleeting and less transient than an illustration in a newspaper."

Kim often incorporated patterns into her illustrations and as her interest grew she started to think about switching over to pattern design. Previously in New York while she was at The Fashion Institute of Technology she was around lots of textile designers and had been interested by what they were doing. Kim began by designing patterns in her spare time, trying to work out which aspect of the field she was most interested in. After ten years of illustrating she made the switch and worked for a couple of textile companies learning how they operated and absorbing how a business is run. "I realised I was really interested in the home décor market and that I wanted to focus on trade rather than licensing my designs or retail".

Kim launched Fayce (her childhood nickname) in 2014. Her studio Is In an old factory in New England. "There are large windows overlooking mountains in the near distance. I feel pretty lucky to be here. It's a small studio but it has enough room for me to roll out fabric. It is not always the neatest but every thing has its place and I like being surrounded by my own work. Having my own space to create is very important, although I do often find myself staring out the windows at the view". The architectural details, materials and old building methods of the factory provide Kim with inspiration, as does the surrounding coast and the vast amount of farmland in the area. "I'm really drawn to history, the contrast of old and new shapes together. I try to simplify those shapes and create a flow, something that moves your eye around a surface, which is what I did as a graphic designer but with typography or images."

Kim tends to make lists and has multiple sketchbooks filled with nothing but lists. "If I'm inspired by a certain part of architecture I'll make a list of what it is exactly that inspires me. From this I will pull out certain words or adjectives and make little abstract pencil drawings based on those adjectives. If it's a cornerstone of a building, I will pick it apart until I find something interesting. Although abstract it will still have hints of the initial elements that caught my eye". Because of her advertising background Kim is very narrative orientated. "It helps me to create new work if I have a story in my head. It doesn't bother me if people don't pick up on that but I hope it produces an emotional response in them." The inspiration for a design will dictate to a certain point the colour pallette used but Kim is naturally drawn to tones and textures that aren't overpowering. "I like colours that are subtle and soft but that have some drama to them".

From her initial pencil drawings, Kim will create detailed charcoal line drawings and those drawings become patterns. They are scanned and the repeats reproduced digitally for wallpaper, turned into silk screens for the fabric or simplified before being embroidered. "I have to tidy up the drawings for embroidery and use cleaner, simpler shapes, the stitches are so literal, it can't be too rough. The embroidery is a similar thought process to printing, but with a different technical process."

Kim started off producing fabrics and wallpaper before she began to incorporate embroidery. She bought an embroidery machine and experimented. "I loved it and became a little obsessed, it was really fun to do quick sketches and then embroider them and see what they looked like as compositions. It was nice to have this quick sketchbook form of embroidery. My machine has a small hoop, when one section is finished I can take it off, move the fabric around and embroider over the top of the piece I have just embroidered, experimenting with overlapping and movement. I can change the composition of the embroidery patterns by moving the hoops. It is a really fun way to play around with the medium, mixing the digital aspect with a hand crafted approach." A lot of the larger pieces are one-offs that Kim will make herself but for particularly substantial orders she brings in help as it can take an entire day to embroider a pillow.

Kim tries to keep her designs simple and abstract whilst evoking something familiar. "When I go though the process of designing any pattern, I know if something is not right; if it's too fussy, too complicated or overworked. When it has depth and movement without feeling chaotic something clicks and I can move forward. These calm patterns have the most impact, and the most longevity.

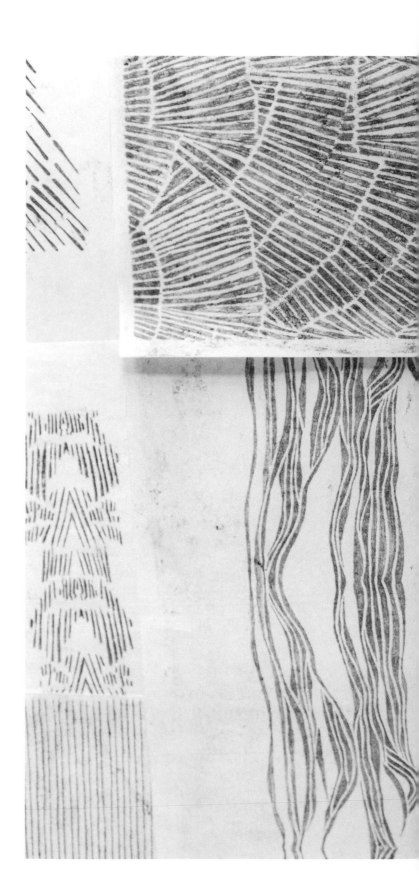

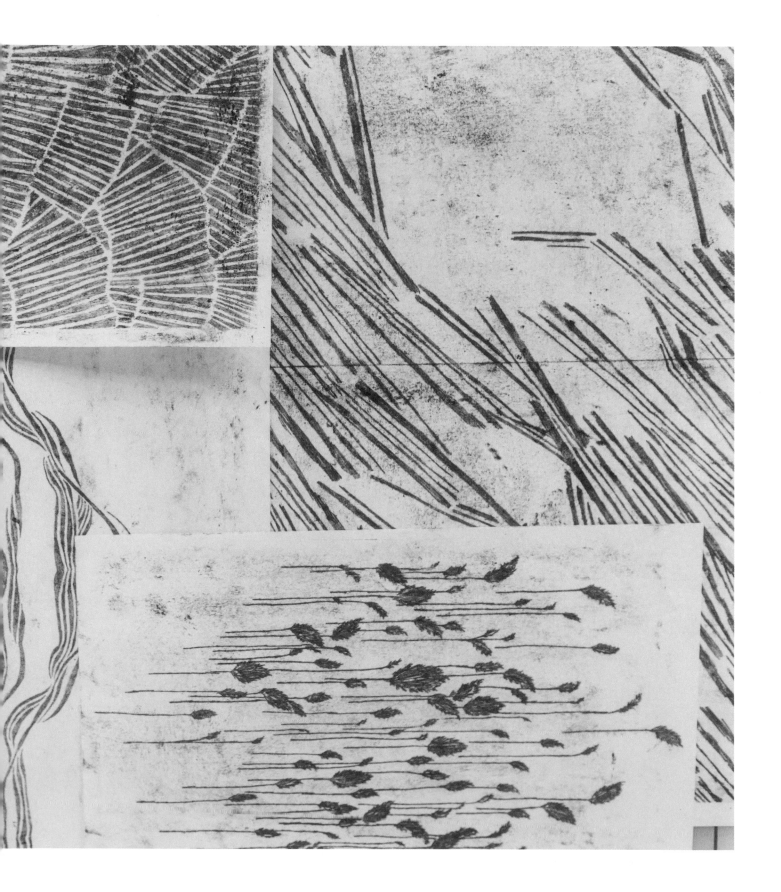

Chapter Three
Patterns in the Home

Pattern At Home

"Our homes in which we seek refuge when our daily toil is over, should beyond all things, afford repose for the mind and body; and that repose can only come with simplicity"
— CFA VOYSEY

Home should be a place of refuge, an escape where our minds can slow down and unwind, a fortress that feels safe and is free from the stresses and fears of the outside world. It should also be a place that represents our personality and feels uniquely ours.

Most of us live in cities, without gardens, in close proximity to our neighbours, who may have a very different sense of what is peaceful. We are separated from the natural world and yet we feel a yearning for it – for the peace and tranquillity it brings. By decorating our homes with botanical patterns and surrounding ourselves with natural imagery we can bring nature inside and emulate a calmer, less urban domestic space.

By hanging curtains with nautical inspired designs at our windows, or covering a plain wall in a pattern created with images of hedgerow flowers, we are seeking out a world that rejuvenates us. Depictions of foliage and flowers, birds, meadows, and the sea can elevate our spirits and remind us of when we felt untroubled. Quiet, calm patterns can give a home a sense of individuality whilst grounding a space without distracting the mind or feeling heavy. Pattern can create an atmospheric backdrop that can form our mismatched possessions into a coherent and pleasing composition.

Many people are afraid of using pattern in their homes, associating the language of pattern with an overbearing, intrusive tone. But pattern is everywhere, whether it is the reflected shadows of a tree on interior walls, the vertical stripes of panelled wood, or the repetitive pattern of bricks. Patterns can be created from anything; a collection of clocks arranged on a wall. A line of carefully gathered feathers from a beach that are proudly displayed by a child, or a wall covered with decorative plates. Curated collections can unintentionally turn into very personal patterns; a connecting theme of something you love that creates a feeling of wellbeing.

Quiet patterns will suit any space, urban or rural, modern or traditional. The delicacy of the lines and the subtle muted tones allow the architecture to speak, the detail of the building will still be visible, not overshadowed by loud, distracting design. Charles Voysey liked to give pattern space. He called the Victorian trend of layering designs "a patterning headache", preferring to pair his patterned wallpaper designs with simple panelled walls. This Victorian advice still applies today. A single favourite pattern, or even a selection of wonderfully mismatched tonal patterns layered together will need space around them to breathe. This in turn will induce a sense of simplicity.

RIGHT Doro wallpaper
by Sidonie

Living Room

The living room is generally where we relax, the visual mood should be soft and comfort is key. With many disparate pieces of furniture, coffee tables, side tables, sofas and chairs, this room can easily look jumbled and cluttered. Pattern can give a focal point. A wallpapered wall behind a sofa can create the colour scheme for a room, or a rug can zone the space linking all of the random pieces of furniture together. Pile sofas with textiles, patterned blankets and throws to wrap up in and plump cushions to sink in to. Frame windows with gently decorated curtains, to create a nurturing environment and to link back to the textiles used on the sofa. Patterns don't need to match. A colour palette that is repeated throughout the room, contrasting designs that enhance one another, or patterns that blend together will create a flow that gives consistency.

LEFT Anna Backlund's living room in Gothenburg, Sweden

Matching Patterns

The practice of having a room of matching wallpaper, curtains and upholstery is becoming more popular again and Birgit Morgensten has a simplified version of this look in her home. A wall of Gräser wallpaper stretches the length of the room, with the large central window framed by curtains of the same fabric. When the curtains are closed the pattern flows across the full wall uninterrupted and when they are open the view outside is framed by the pattern. The simple upholstery and white walls stop the matching pattern being overwhelming creating a very peaceful room.

Leading off from this space is a little reading area. Birgit found the two little stools in the street and reupholstered them in different prints of her fabrics. "I wanted to place them next to each other, and keep a harmonious colour theme, but the shades are varied to keep it more interesting".

Layered Patterns

Layering pattern upon pattern needn't create the "patterning headache" Voysey refers to. By keeping the colour tones in a similar palette, the designs can blend into each other, creating layers of warmth without feeling cluttered. In my living room, I already had Brambleweb wallpaper on the wall and had recently upholstered my 1950's sofa in Bird linen for a shoot. I was worried that afterwards I would have to redecorate, that they would be too much together but the watercolour pink tones in Bird, reflected the pink tinged grey of Brambleweb and the difference in scale between the patterns mean they stand alone without being isolated. And mixing monochrome patterns and furniture with contrasting designs in soft colours will also add atmosphere and warmth.

Daniel Heath's living room is an eclectic mix of Daniel's designs, blended in with vintage pieces. The small space could be chaotic but a tiny sofa has been chosen to nestle into an alcove to maximise space and mustard tones run throughout. The textures of the rug and the woven sofa keep the room interesting and the warm hues of the wooden sofa, table and shelf tie the space together. Daniel says, "I am trying to be a bit more curated in the things that I select. You can end up with a hotchpotch of stuff, which can be charming, but living in a small space in London I have to be restrained. London is busy and frenetic as it is and our house is becoming more of a refuge from that busyness, and the hectic pace of everyday life."

Relaxed

Shannan Camanaro's love of the ocean is clear to see in the seating area of her urban loft in New York. The watery coastal blues of the Eskayel wallpaper are echoed in the super laidback blue leather sofa. "It's always scary to commit to a pattern because the idea of a clean blank wall is so appealing but once you commit and then you see pictures of the bare wall without the pattern it looks so cold and unfinished. Pattern can really complete a room and it's ok to mix it up." She says. The assorted patterns in varying tones of blue are mixed with a shaggy cream rug and faux fur throw, adding layers of comfort and texture to make this a space that invites lounging.

The timeless blue and white colour scheme of Emma Von Bromsen's living room is a classic combination. Emma's crane design is used as wallpaper on the walls and again on the cushions. This could look too matchy-matchy but by mixing in her mackerel design and a patterned throw, the room becomes modern and relaxed. The rich indigo tones of the textiles keep the overall appearance cohesive and the linen of the traditional sofa has a comfortable lived in look, the plain natural colourway gives space to the intensity of the patterns making for a very restful room.

Upholstery

When Kim Rosen is designing patterns for Fayce she tries to picture what she would want in her own house. "I like things that are not overpowering I don't want something to be a focal point. I like décor to blend in with my stuff. I have a variety of different types of pieces in my home that don't necessarily go together but they all work because there is a subtle palette." She keeps things neutral with the occasional pop of colour. Mixing patterns to an extent but not too many crazy designs together. This accent chair upholstered in Gather has been paired with a vintage rug but as the rest of the furnishings and décor are so simple the look is restrained.

Monochrome

Vanessa & Brendan of Mineheart live in a 1960's house and have added a bit of cosiness and warmth to the clean lines of the architecture with their Almost White wallpaper. Their Loveletter wallpaper behind the faded leather sofa has a sense of history to it; the pattern consists of elegant hand written love notes from a bygone era, a rarity in these days of email and text messages. The romantic time worn charm adds a sense of stillness to their home, emphasised by the combination of distressed leather sofa and their contemporary take on traditional cushion designs. The open plan space is zoned with three different monochrome wallpapers, all lined up next to each other but defined by the wide central chimney breast. The seating area here has a romantic faded damask design, happily contrasted with the clean lines of the furniture but the space is unified by the monochrome pattern in the decorative rug on the floor, which brings the room together with a repetitive curation of delicate pattern. "We generally like walls to be quite bright and white," says Brendan. "With dark patterned walls you feel like you can't hang anything on top, that isn't the case with the bleached out versions of these designs, they make the house feel light. We like wood and natural materials but if you mix that with pattern and too many other materials, it becomes too much. Our style is quite simple."

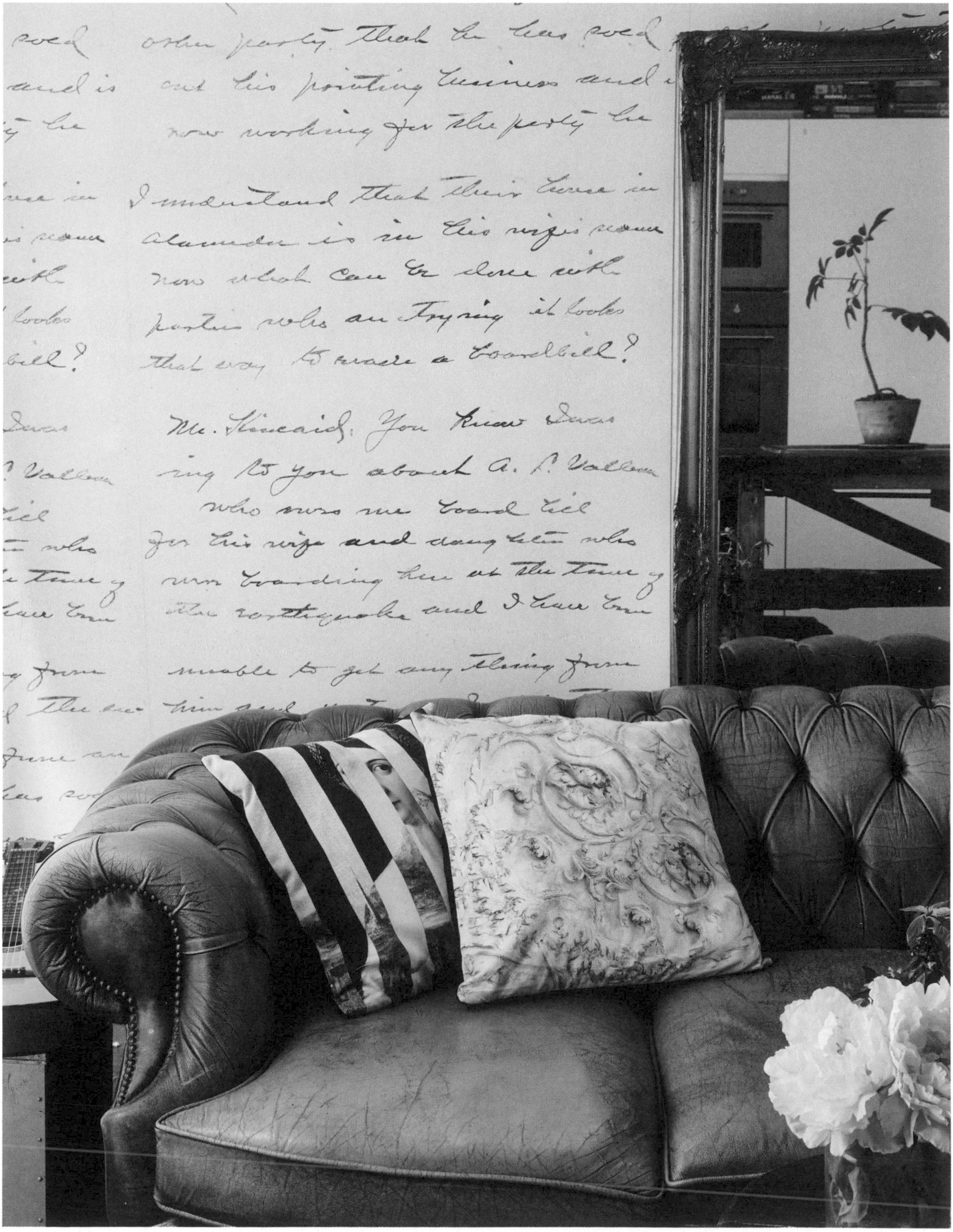

Kitchen and Dining

As we live in increasingly open plan spaces, the kitchen is often at the centre, a multipurpose space, and a place of community where we can be sociable and entertain. A kitchen is no longer a purely utilitarian space and pattern can help demonstrate this, changing the mood from practical to homely, it also serves a functional purpose in hiding wear and tear in areas that get heavy use. You may want to define the different uses for your kitchen, which can be done with pattern, either permanently with different patterned floor tiles, one design for the eating area and another for the cooking zones. Or fluidly, by adding a patterned tablecloth and napkins to a dining table, you can spontaneously transform the mood from temporary office to food preparation station to a relaxed dinner for friends. Pattern can inspire, conversation, ideas and creativity.

Bespoke

This family kitchen in Kensal Rise in London (*on previous page*) has been given bespoke treatment with Daniel Heath's Espalier laser etched slate tiles running the length of the wooden units. The extremely detailed etched Jaybirds sitting on gnarled apple branches contrast beautifully with the raw timeworn patina of the reclaimed Welsh slate and add a wistful timelessness to what is a very practical kitchen.

Hand painted

Norwegian artist Ida Helland Hanson hand painted the walls of her families 1860's timber house on the edge of a fjord using a modern interpretation of traditional Norwegian paint effects in what was originally a workshop space. In times gone past it was usual for people in Norway to paint walls with their own imagery, especially in churches. Ida uses more subtle methods than is traditional with subdued, unusual tones and organic imagery. "It is free association painting, but it is also practical. I painted the clouds on the ceiling as a way of making the room lighter but still showing the original wood. I was planning to do the pattern all over but it takes so much time and I thought that the pattern looked like a cloud so they became clouds. The apple tree was painted to cover a damaged bit of wood. I used some of the same pattern in the ceiling to tie it together." Says Ida. The gentle chalky pastel colours she has used contrast beautifully with the warmth of the wooden walls and antique table and the simplicity of the modern chairs and are reflected in the contemporary glass splash back that she has also painted.

Colour Theme

In a fast paced world gathering around a table with friends or family is a calming ritual. Whilst we may not go to the ceremony of matching tablecloths, placemats and napkins very often anymore, using some of these elements can create a sense of occasion, making guests feel special and also tie the table in with your room décor, even for an everyday dinner. Birgit Morgensten does this with her hand printed textiles and has created her own tablecloths, napkins and wallpaper especially for her home. Using contrasting designs in the adjoining kitchen and dining room but with complimentary colours, a blue green colour scheme in the kitchen moves across to a deep blue in the dining room with screen-printed cushion covers to complement the scheme. This could feel overwhelming but the rooms are large and there is so much space around and between these patterns that the feeling is contemporary, spacious and bright. "I like to take one colour for one room, I theme accessories to that colour in varying shades, keeping possessions and colours fairly minimal, it creates a feeling of calm unification," says Birgit.

Details

If you prefer a simple functional space, small pops of pattern on ceramics and accessories can add a little personality to the room. Getting them out when you feel like it and hiding the pattern away in cupboards when you don't. This little mismatched tea setting in my kitchen has sentimental value to me. The Marimekko bowl by Sanna Annukka was a present from my cousin; the Design House Stockholm milk jug was a present from my Mum and the little feathered bird vessels, used as cups were made in collaboration with Muck Ceramics. Rebecca Hernandez of Muck handmade the pots and I hand painted each one. Despite all the various patterns the monochrome palette and simple shapes ensure they all work together and the plain white 1960's Rosenthal coffee pot that was a wedding gift to my parents in the 60's tones down the pattern mix.

A collection of photographs and illustrations on the wall of Anna Backlund's kitchen set off her knitted cushion designs for House of Rym, adding playful colour and pattern to an otherwise functional kitchen. The knitted and woven textures of the cushions contrast with the graphic black table and a patterned mug and the cosy outfits of some of Anna's illustrated characters echo the colours of the cushions. These can all be changed whenever Anna feels like it with out permanent commitment.

Hannah Nunn's kitchen is a simple space with small hints of colour and subtle pattern. "I only have a small flat so there are limitations on how many things I can have. I love art and pattern but I also really love a clean space. I like small accents of pattern, be that in a tea towel or how things look next to each other creating their own patterns by association", explains Hannah. Her kitchen table exemplifies this, with a row of delicate ceramic spoons made by Justine Allison hanging in a stripe on the wall and tea served in textured patterned mugs in pebble shades. A monochrome simple print on a vintage enamel light enhances this small, subtle selection of items.

Hallway

Entrance hallways are often neglected spaces but they should be welcoming, friendly and warm, a frequently tiny room that conjures thoughts of what lies beyond. Whereas corridors and stairs are transitional spaces, often passed through fairly quickly without lingering, creating a division between the public and private spaces of a home. There is enormous scope to use bolder patterns in these often-narrow spaces than you would normally as people rarely dawdle in a hallway, spending a relatively short period of time engaging with the decoration. Hallways are a good place to use pattern creatively, boldness with out brashness, maybe a large-scale monochrome mural with hand drawn lines and intricate detail creating a transition from one space to the next.

LEFT Botanica wallpaper in Emma Von Bromssen's house in Gothenburg, Sweden

Floors

Birgit Morgensten has painted a classic grey and white tile design on to her wooden floorboards. Not only does this pattern make the room seem larger it adds personality to a white painted entrance hall and guides her guests through the house, creating a directional flow between the different routes leading off the main hall.

I have wallpapered a set of stairs in my apartment. The slightly shabby distressed wood on the stairs worked well with the fairy tale feel of the gnarly branches in my Oak Tree design. The pattern is contained within each stair tread so the hallway still feels spacious and uncluttered with the illustrative design contained within little pockets of subtle colour. These have been papered in a temporary way, using wallpaper offcuts and I can swap them for another design when I feel like it.

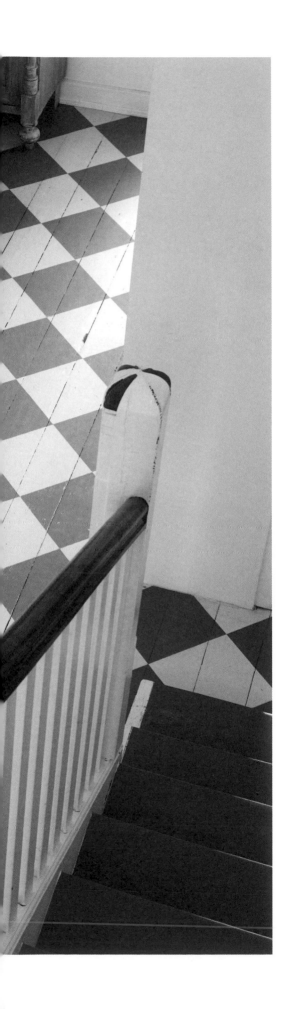

Walls

Blue and white is an absolutely classic colour combination, all hues of blue work with every shade of white and the structured marks in Fayce's wallpaper design, Lapel shown in Kim Rosen's hallway have a very fresh almost tailored feel with a slightly nautical edge. "An accent wall in wallpaper can have a huge impact even if it is on a tiny section of wall", says Kim. The disciplined formation within the design and the clean white negative space creates a framework of harmonious order that works well in the room. "We have a small house and I like everything to be tidy and orderly. An orderly house with calm designs means that I can think better".

Bedroom

This is the room to allow yourself to unwind, to recharge and rest. Whether you like to go to bed early or in the small hours we all want to wake up feeling energised and rejuvenated. A bedroom should be serene and harmonious, a comforting, nurturing space where you can totally shut off from the outside world and relax. Pattern can be used all over, or in details such as bed linen and throws, textiles that can easily be swapped around or stored out of the way depending on how you are feeling or how cold it is. Some people will only sleep in white cotton, whilst others prefer to snuggle up in patchwork vintage quilts, or throws bought whilst travelling that have sentimental memories. Display anything that makes you feel good. Try to use patterns that don't compete with each other, create a dialogue between the different designs so that each one will relate to the other, whether that is through, tones, shapes or scale.

Brick

I have never been very good at sleeping and have suffered from insomnia on and off for years so I like to sleep in a very calm uncluttered bedroom. But I don't like rooms to look cold so I have used quite a few patterns to bring in warmth but they are all subtle. The most noticeable thing about the room is the brick wall, which acts as a textured backdrop bringing the different pattern designs together, which are mostly monochrome. Bird wallpaper with small-scale feathers is on one wall. A traditional oriental rug design is printed on to a rug manufactured from wooden blocks by Seletti, the wooden material keeps the look modern and blends into the wooden floorboards. Next to an old fireplace is a very basic Ikea chair that has been covered with Briar Owl wallpaper, which gives tiny hints of illustrative pattern and in the old hearth are concrete Flaster tiles by Ivanka, the motif design is traditional but made using a contemporary material. This combination of raw textures and monochrome patterns add softness to what could be a masculine space. On the only plain wall an inherited cupboard has been lined with a very soft white and pale grey snowflake design. The individual patterns in the room are not isolated from each other, but are given their own space without competing.

Paper Folds

Mineheart's Paper Palace Folded Hall wallpaper mural gives Vanessa and Brendan's bedroom a sense of grandeur. They collaborated with paperwork artist Simon Schubert to create the illusion of a Baroque interior. The disorientating perspective of the intricate paper folds creates a mysterious yet strangely calming atmosphere. The fairly minimal space is uncluttered and bright and the tranquillity is paired with a sense of playfulness in the surreal Mineheart pendant lamps and elegant vintage chair. Vanessa likes to mix different styles and materials together, preferring an eclectic mix with few patterns but the ones that are used stand out.

Calm Textiles

After turning their front room into a
bedroom Daniel Heath printed his
Eastern Peacocks design in bespoke
colours especially for that room to suit
the materials that were already in there.
The grey of the walls was used as the
base colour for the wallpaper and the
copper detailing of the peacocks to mirror
the copper curtain rails. "I wanted to
reflect those colours and to add a bit of
narrative to the room. We used to have
curtains in here too but I didn't want the
wallpaper and curtains fighting, you need
to give the patterns space." Everything
else in the room is quite paired back, the
prints on the cushions are tone on tone
and the throw is textured in similar hues
leaving the wallpaper to speak. The old
Victorian hearth has also been given a
little bit of pattern with an art deco design
of Daniel's etched on to slate tiles. The
design is geometric and quite bold but
the tonal aspect of the slate means that
it doesn't distract. "I don't think my art
deco collection in bright colours would
work in here, it would blow everything else
out, whereas at the moment the colours
are balanced. We wanted it to feel quite
ethereal and light, it's nice to wake up
feeling calm."

Multipurpose

Hannah Nunn has maximised space in her large bedroom, zoning out different areas using pattern. Her Meadow Grass wallpaper behind the bed defines the sleeping space. Next to this is a large window with views over treetops. Rather than waste this empty area that gets dappled in sunshine, Hannah has kept the space flexible by creating a little seating nook here using upholstered chairs in Paper Meadow where she likes to read, think and practise her ukulele. On the far side of the room is a storage area, marked

by yet another pattern, this time Charlotte's Garden wallpaper. The similarly chalky soft hued colours used in all the patterns means there is no clashing, they all gently work together creating a very soothing mood. Hannah says, "Even my most subtle patterns might be too much if they were used around a whole room. I have simple tastes and want simplicity in my home. Nothing too complicated or busy, I try to set things off in their best environment, give a pattern or object some space even if it is something tiny".

Bathroom

Bathrooms can often be cold, blank spaces, usually white and the perfect place on which to stamp your personality. This very functional, often masculine room is frequently neglected and can easily be softened by just adding some soft patterned towels, an interesting shower curtain, or a vintage rug, or, if you prefer smaller items, a mix and match selection of vessels for soap, cotton wool and toothbrushes. Minimal decoration can be created simply without too dramatic a commitment, even the way plain white bathroom tiles are arranged, whether in a herringbone design, brick or a grid can change the look of the room, making the bathroom appear industrial or more luxurious. Or, add textures that already have a patina, like marble surfaces creating natural pattern. Having a bath is the most common way to relax so it makes sense to create a beautiful serene space to relax in.

Bespoke Elegance

This beautiful bathroom in North London (*on previous page*) features delicate hand drawn birds and intricate vines etched in a continuous pattern along all four walls of the room across different surfaces by Daniel Heath. The etched mirror on one wall emphasises the space of the room as well as reflecting the patterns on the white wood ash back again at a different scale, which change depending on the angle that it is viewed from. With the addition of the elegantly carved marble basin the room is a serene and highly luxurious space.

Rustic Nature

My bathroom was decorated at the end of a long renovation process when the budget had run out. The plain white bathroom furniture and the Victorian cupboard were ebay finds. The tile mural was a way of creating interest and adding personality to my bathroom whilst also serving a practical purpose. The fine lines of the dragonflies and twigs create a gentle effect, adding femininity and balance to the modernity of a classic white sink and the nature inspired design goes with the cupboard that I painted and adapted to hold the sink. Dragonfly mural is a nod to the historical mural but used in a contemporary way.

Small Space

William Morris was a fan of large-scale wallpapers covering the walls of small rooms so he would have appreciated this shower room wallpapered entirely in Eskayel's soothing watery blue design. The pattern is quite bold and creates a strong impact but the calming blues make it serene and tranquil and when paired with white ceilings, woodwork and shower curtain the effect is spacious and bright.

Index

Acknowledgements

Huge thank you to my friend and brilliant photographer Alun Callender for agreeing to shoot this book. As always you totally understood my vision and your enthusiasm made the shoots such a pleasure.

Thanks to Catharine at Clearview for having faith in my idea and for being so tolerant of my creative stubbornness. Thanks to Charlotte Heal for patiently listening to me and making this book beautiful.

I am extremely grateful to all the designers that so graciously let us into their homes and studios, it was such a privilege to talk to each of them about their designs and how they work, without their generosity this book would not exist.

A very big thank you to my Mum who painstakingly read through every passage I had written educating me about grammar as she did so.

I wish I could thank the delightfully charismatic Simon Midgley who had been planning the PR for this book before he was so tragically taken from this world. Finally thank you to all my wonderful customers and clients around the world, I am extremely thankful for your loyalty and custom and I hope this book inspires you and encourages you to fill your homes with quiet pattern.

For more pattern inspiration follow me on Instagram @abigailjedwards

Bibliography

CFA Voysey — Arts and Crafts Designer
by Karen Livingstone with
Max Donnelly and Linda Parry
V&A Publishing 2016

William Morris Textiles by Linda Parry
George Weidenfeld & Nicholson Ltd 1983

Scandinavian Design
by Charlotte & Peter Fell
Taschen 2002

Stig Lindberg, Swedish Artist & Designer
by Dag Widman & Berndt Klyvare
Rabén & Sjögren Stockholm 1962

Edward Bawden & His Circle
by Malcolm Yorke
Antique Collectors' Club

Some Hints on Pattern Designing
by William Morris
The Architect 1881

Patterns in Interior Environments —
Perception, Psychology and Practice
By Patricia Rodemann
John Wiley & Sons Inc 1999

Patterns for Post-War Britain — The Tile
designs of Peggy Angus by Katie Arber
Middlesex University Press MoDA 2002

Is Mr Ruskin Living Too Long — Selected
writings of EW Godwin on Victorian
Architecture, Design & Culture
by Juliet Kinchin and Paul Stirton
White Cockade Publishing 2005

Design Edward Bawden Eric Ravilious
by Saffron Walden
The Fry Art Gallery 2003

Eric Ravilious Design
by Brian Webb & Peyton Skipwith
ACC Art Books 2015

Edward Bawden Storyteller
Morley Gallery London 2014

Modern Danish Textiles
by Bent Salicath & Arne Karlsen
The Danish Society of Arts & Crafts 1959

Swedish Design by Denise Hagströmer
The Swedish Institute 2000

Bawden, Ravilious and the
Artists of Great Bardfield
by Gill Saunders and Malcolm Yorke
The V&A. 2015

ABOVE Anna Backlund's garden
room, in Gothenburg Sweden

Resources

Featured Designers

Abigail Edwards
abigailedwards.com

Birgit Morgenstern
birgitmorgenstern.se

Daniel Heath
danielheath.co.uk

Emma Von Bromssen
emmavonbromssen.se

Eskayel
eskayel.com

Fayce Textiles
faycetextiles.com

Hannah Nunn
hannahnunn.co.uk

House Of Rym
houseofrym.com

Mineheart
mineheart.com

Rebecca Atwood
rebeccaatwood.com

Sidonie
sidoniestudio.com

Source List

Bemz
bemz.com

Blithfield
blithfield.co.uk

Boras Tapeter
borastapeter.se

Common Room
commonroom.co

Design House Stockholm
designhousestockholm.com

Engblad & Co
eco.se

Ikea
ikea.com

Marimekko
marimekko.com

Morris & Co
stylelibrary.com

Muck Ceramics
muckceramics.com

St Judes
stjudesfabrics.co.uk

Trustworth
trustworth.com

Window Film
windowfilm.co.uk

Shops That are Filled with Quiet Pattern

Anthropologie
anthropologie.com

Heals
heals.com

ABC Carpet & Home
abchome.com

Leadbetter & Good
leadbetterandgood.com

Skandium
skandium.com

Conran Shop
conranshop.co.uk

About the Author

Abigail began her career studying art at Wimbledon School of Art in London and the École des Beaux-Arts in Paris. After a brief stint assisting in galleries in New York, a passion for interiors took over and she returned to London to style shoots and write about interiors for a diverse range of editorial and commercial clients; such as Ikea, The White Company, Marks & Spencer, Harrods, *The Sunday Times*, *The Guardian*, *House & Garden* and *Country Living* amongst many others. She was also Deputy Decorating Editor at *Country Homes & Interiors* magazine for several years.

Abigail launched her first wallpaper collection in 2011, the award winning, hand drawn designs now grace the walls of homes and commercial spaces around the world.

Published in the UK in 2018 by Clearview Books
22 Clarendon Gardens, London W9 1AZ
www.clearviewbooks.com

© Text: Abigail Edwards
© Compilation: Clearview Books
© Photography: Alun Callender
© Photography: p16, 25 Trustworth Studios, USA; p19, 21, 22, 23, 24 Morris & Co, Style Library UK; p27, 29, 30- St Judes, UK. Courtesy of Victoria & Albert Museum; p28 Common Room, UK. Courtesy of Victoria & Albert Museum; p31 Blithfield, UK; p33, 35, 36, 37, 38, 39 Boråstapeter, Sweden; p34 Bemz, Sweden; p40, 66, 68, 70, 112 Middleimage; p124 Emma Von Brömssen, Sweden; p67 Engblad & Co, Sweden; 78, 79, 80, 82, 112, 139 Eskayel, USA; p84, 85, 86, 87, 88 Jessie Cowan, USA; p90, 91, 92, 95 Tory Williams, USA; p96, 97, 98, 100, 113 (right), 127 (right) Chattman Photography, USA; 105 Sidonie, USA; p116, 137 Tom Fallon, UK

A CIP record of this book is available from the British Library.
ISBN: 978-1908337-450

Design: Charlotte Heal Design
Editor and copy editor: Catharine Snow
Production: Simonne Waud

Printed in Italy by Graphicom S.r.l.
Colour reproduction by XY Digital, London